THE GANDHAVAMSA

(A HISTORY OF PALI LITERATURE)

Editor
BIMALENDRA KUMAR
M.A. (Pali & Buddhist Studies), M. Phil., Ph.D. (Delhi),
Lecturer in Indo-Tibetan Studies,
Visva-Bharati, Santiniketan (W.B.)

Eastern Book Linkers

DELHI :: (INDIA)

B.E. 2535 1992 E. C. V.B. 2047

Published by
EASTERN BOOK LINKERS
5825, New Chandrawal, Jawahar Nagar,
Delhi-110007

First Edition : 1992

ISBN—81-85133-58-1

Printed by :

Amar Printing Press (Sham Printing Agency).
8/25, Vijay Nagar, Double Storey, Delhi-110009

गंध-वंसो

सम्पादक
डॉ० बिमलेन्द्र कुमार
एम० ए० (द्वय); एम० फिल०; पी० एच०-डी० (दिल्ली),
प्राध्यापक, इण्डो-तिब्बतन अध्ययन विभाग,
विश्व-भारती, शान्तिनिकेतन (प० बं०)

ईस्टर्न बुक लिंकर्स
दिल्ली :: (भारत)

बुद्धाब्द २५३३ ईस्वी १९९२ विक्रमाब्द २०४७

ईस्टर्न बुक लिंकर्स
५८२५, न्यू चन्द्रावल, जवाहर नगर, दिल्ली-७

प्रथम संस्करण : १९९२

ISBN—81-85133-58-1

मुद्रक :
अमर प्रिंटिंग प्रैस (शाम प्रिंटिंग एजेंसी),
८/२५ डबल स्टोरी, विजय नगर, दिल्ली-९

FOREWORD

The *Gandhavamsa* is an important text in the *Vaṃsa*-literature. It presents a brief account related to the origin and development of Pali literature in India and neighbouring countries from the sixth century B.C. till the end of the seventeenth century A.D. It, in this way, serves a most valuable cause in introducing the Pali text from hoary past and their stages of development. A very beautiful picture of the scholars who contributed towards the development of Pali literature, may be seen through it. In this way, though it is a small book, it is very important in furnishing the continuous flow of development of Pali literature.

It is a matter of great satisfaction that Pali is being taught at different levels in University education. Students are also taking interest in going deep into the original sources for having a clear understanding of the various concepts. Sometimes, they are found enquisitive to know the historical development of the Pali literature. They also seek information about an original text dealing with the problem. As a fulfilment of such enquiries, it was planned to bring out a critical edition of the *Gandhavaṃsa*, a treatise dealing with the history of books. Dr. Bimalendra Kumar has taken up this issue and making right efforts in preparing the critical edition of the text, has brought out the text with exhaustive introduction. He deserves my heartly congratulations for his commendable work.

Today, I am really glad to have the critical edition of the *Gandhavaṃsa* with its introduction. I have belief in the potentiality of Dr. Bimalendra Kumar and hope that he will continue his efforts in bringing out the critical edition of the useful Pali texts in future. I bless him for his bright future and a peaceful life devoted to preserving the Pali tradition in India.

MAHESH TIWARY
Professor of Buddhist Studies,
Deptt. of Buddhist studies,
University of Delhi,
Delhi—1100007

PREFACE

The idea of preparing a critical edition of the small Pali text came to me, when I submitted my thesis for Ph.D. course in 1989. After having pondered over the materials, I found that the *Gandhavaṃsa* is small non-canonical text, which is immensely useful for research scholars and students. A plan, accordingly, was thought to prepare a critical edition of this text in Devanāgari script with an exhaustive introduction in English. I transcribed this text from Roman script into Devanāgari script in 1989 itself. But, every thing takes shape at its own time of fruition, guided by some unseen action force. Due to some circumstances, I remained engaged in other academic and research activities and could not find time to devote myself for editing of this text. In the beginning of last year, the editing of this text was started under the noble guidance of Prof. Mahesh Tiwary.

The *Gandhavaṃsa* had been edited in Roman characters for the first time by Professor Minayeff of St. Petersburg and was published in the Journal of Pali Text Society (J.P.T.S.) for the year 1886. The text was found in Burma and had been edited with the help of two manuscripts, written in Burmese character. The first manuscript contained besides the Pali text a translation into Burmese. It belonged to the author of the translation—the monk U-Khyen or Muninda, at Schwedowg, near Prome. It consisted of twenty-seven leaves. The second manuscript contained twelve leaves and only Pali text without translation. It was full of clerical errors. The Roman edition of the text was mainly based upon the first manuscript. The additions of another manuscript, being corrupted, were given in the foot notes.

In course of editing in the Devanagari script, the varients, which were more helpful in clarifying the meaning of the concepts, were adjusted in the body of the text and rests have been included in the foot-notes. I am really grateful to the editor, for utilizing the text for making the present one more useful and accessible.

Attempt has been made to make the text understandable to modern mind, more acquainted with new techniques of research activities. For the purpose, the name of the chapter and the main subjects discussed theirin have been indicated first. Thereafter, the details of the contents have been exhibited under the headings and sub-headings with different size of letters. The verses of the text have been numbered serially. Punctuations as accepted in modern technique of editing and specially as followed in the publication of the critical edition of Pali *Tipitaka* and *Aṭṭhakathas* by Nava Nālandā Mahāvihāra, Nālandā, has faithfully been followed in this text. In the margin, the page numbers of the Roman version of the text have been given with the abbreviated symbol R. It is for easy reference to this version as well as for the critical awareness of the various readings.

There is an introduction in the begining, discussing some of the basic problems, presenting brief account of the contents of each chapter. It has been done with a view to introduce the text as a whole to the readers. In the end, two indexes have been appended namely; the index of the verses and index of important words, appearing in the text.

On this pions moment, I take this opportunity to express my gratitude to Prof. Mahesh Tiwary, Professor of Buddhist Studies, Deptt. of Buddhist Studies, Delhi University, Deihi, whose unfailing erudite guidance and inspiring zeal for the search of knowledge, made this book available in Devanagari script. He has been generous enough to write the foreword of this book and for which I also express my ever indebtedness to him.

I was also given useful informations and helpful advices in their classes and in informal discussions by my other teachers, Prof. Sanghsen Singh, Prof. K.K. Mittal. Dr. (Ms.) Sudhasen Gupta, Ms. Latika Lahiri, Dr. Bhikkhu Satyapal, Dr. G.G. Gyatso and Shri H.P. Gangnegi. To all of them, I acknowledge with thanks indebtedness. Prof. Biswanath Banerjee, Rtd. Head of the Deptt. of Sanskrit & Pali, Visva-Bharati, Santiniketan, Prof. L.N. Tiwary, Head of the Deptt. of Pali & Theravada, Sampoornananda Sanskrit University, Varanasi. Dr. N.H. Samtani (Varanasi) have been the source of making right efforts in my day-to-day academic and research activities. I am also thankful to Shri Suniti Kumar Pathak and Lama Chimpajee, Deptt. of Indo-Tibetan Studies, Visva-Bharti, Santiniketan for their noble suggestions and discussions.

I am grateful to my seniors like Dr. Baidyanath Labh, Lecturer, Deptt. of Buddhist Studies, University of Jammu, Dr. Arun Kumar Sinha, Dr. Amar Nath Thakur, Dr. Om Prakash Pathak, Dr. Satyendra Kumar Pandey extending to me valuable suggestions in preparing materials for the present book. Simultaneously, I feel obliged to all my friends and *Katyāṇamitras*, especially to Dr. Sudhir Kumar Dixit, Shri K.K. Singh, Shri V.M. Chaudhary, Shri S.K. Pandey, Shri Sanjay Tripathy, Shri K.K. Pandey, Shri Rajeeva Kumar, Dr. N.K. Das, Dr. Bhabashankar Mukherjee and others for their most useful academic cooperation and suggestions.

I express the deep sense of gratitude to my parents, whose perennial inspirations, ever-abiding love, care and blissful blessings, all cooperated to give my ideas a concrete shape. I also feel indebted to other members of the family and relatives, who always inspired me to pursue my academic sojourn.

Now, I would like to express my heartiest and affectionate thanks to my wife Mrs. Rekha (Meenu), whose manifested cooperation made the completion of the work.

And finally to Shri Sham Lal Malhotra, Proprietor, Eastern Book Linkers, Delhi, and Shri Hiralaljee of Amar Pritting Press, Delhi, for their unfailing cooperation in the publication of the present volume in time.

Lastly, I humbly crave indulgence of learned scholars for any error of fact or judgement or lapse that may have crept in the present work.

Santiniketan, BIMALENDRA KUMAR
February 8, 1992.

ABBREVIATIONS

A.N.	*Aṅguttaranikāya* (Nalanda Edition)
Asl.	*Aṭṭhasālinī* (Ed. P.V. Bapat & R.D. Wadekar)
D.N.	*Dīghanikāya* (Nalanda Edition)
G.V.	*Gandhavaṃsa* (Present Volume)
K.N.	*Khuddakanikāya* (Nalanda Edition)
M.N.	*Majjhimanikāya* (Nalanda Edition)
R	Roman
S.S.	*Saddhammasaṅgaha* (Nalanda Edition)
S.V.	*Sumaṅgalavilāsinī* (Nalanda Edition)
म० 1	First Burmese Manuscript
म० 2	Second Burmese Manuscript

विसय-उद्देसो

INTRODUCTION

A. VAMSA - LITERATURE

Vaṃsa[1] - literature is one of the chief characteristics of Pāli literature. Although, there is no any text with the name of *Vaṃsa* in the literature of Sanskrit language or any other Old-Indo-Aryan language, but in the Brāhmaṇas texts of Vedic literature, there is a piece named *Vaṃsa - Brāhmaṇa* in which there is a description of tradition of Brāhmaṇa - ācāryas. There is a well known old-text named '*Harivaṃśa-Purāṇa*'. In some of the chapters of *Bṛhdāraṇyaka-upaniṣad*, there is the mention of the tradition of special spiritual knowledge of saints. As for example, in the sixth *Brāhmaṇa* of the second chapter of this *upaniṣad*, there is the description of *vaṃsa* of *madhukāṇda* or the tradition of *Madhu-vidyā*. And in the sixth *Brāhmaṇa* of *Yajñavalkīya-Kāṇḍa*, there is the mention of detailed *Vaṃsa* tradition. Again, what has been called *Itihāsa-purāṇa* in the *Chāndogya-upaniṣad*, can be compared with Pāli *Vaṃsa*-texts in the sense of subject and style. The difference between *Itihāsa-purāṇa* and *Vaṃsa*-texts is that *Purāṇa* is the mainly old sayings where as the Pāli *Vaṃsa*-texts deal with more history than sayings. According to Indian tradition, there are

---

1 The literal meaning of the word *Vaṃsa* is bamboo, race, lineage, family, tradition, hereditory, custom, usage, reputation, dynasty etc. It is stated as a certain game in the enumeration of pastimes and tricks. *Vaṃsa* also means "chronicles" or "history" of a race, of a dynasty, of a line of teachers, etc. Hence, any history, going back to the earliest beginings in the titles such as *Buddhavaṃsa, Dīpavaṃsa, Mahāvaṃsa, Thūpavaṃsa*, etc.

five characteristics of *Purāṇa* and *Itihāsa-purāṇa*,[2] namely *sarga, pratisarga, vaṃsa, manvantara* and *vaṃśānucarita*. The last two are very important with respect to our present study. The *Viṣṇu, Vāyu, Matsya, Bhāgavata*, all the *Purāṇas* deal with the detailed *vaṃsa*-tradition of the dynasty. The Pāli *vaṃsa*-literature also explains the same but it is little bit more historical than that of *Mahābhārata* and *Purāṇas*. In Pāli *vaṃsa*-literature, the history of the Buddha has been dealt with and in this context, there is also the tradition of the teachers of *saddhama*.

The Indians have never distinguished between myths, legends, history and historiography. In India there had always been merely a type of epical poems. So the Buddhists too considered all the legends about the Buddha of the former ages and previous births of Gotama Buddha in the *Buddhavaṃsa*, in the *Cariyāpiṭaka* and in the *Jātaka*-book as also the whole of the Buddha legend to be history. The monks of Ceylon narrated in the historical sections of the Aṭṭhakathas too the history of the introduction of Buddhism into the island according to the pattern and model of these legendary poems and deriving the same from them. They invented legends that would connect the Buddhists community of Ceylon not only with that of India, but even with the Buddha himself-edifying legends, in which was told as to how the exalted one visited the island, that is that age was inhabited only by demons and snake gods, flew over to it in the company of gods to let the light of his teachings shine forth there and to prepare for the future greatness of the church of Ceylon. Holy legends of this type led to the mythical accounts about the early kings of Ceylon and further to semi-historical accounts concerning Aśoka, Mahinda, the Councils and the transmission of the holy texts to the island. The closer these records go to the historical age, the more prominent begin to become the real historical accounts, without the legends having receded wholly into the background. To the tradition of the church were added popular

---

2 *"Sargaśca pratisargaśca vaṃśo manvantarāṇi ca, Vaṃśānucaritaṃ caiva purāṇaṃ pañcalakkhaṇaṃ* -- quoted in *Pāli Sāhitya kā Itihāsa*, by Bharat Singh Upadhyaya, p.655.

secular narratives and anecdotes. So, the historical sections of the Aṭṭhakathas, that are by now already lost to us, of which the subject-matter described here, has been deduced only from the available Pali chronicles and commentaries, became as it were the store-house of spiritual and secular traditions of all kinds and also of real historical accounts.[3]

There are mainly fifteen books in the *Vaṃsa*-literature. They are - *1. Dīpavaṃsa, 2. Mahāvaṃsa, 3. Cūlavaṃsa, 4. Buddhaghosuppatti, 5. Saddhammasaṅgaha, 6. Mahābodhivaṃsa, 7. Thūpavaṃsa, 8. Attanagaluvihāravaṃsa, 9.Dāthāvaṃsa, 10. Chakesadhātuvaṃsa, 11. Nalāṭadhātuvaṃsa, 12. Sandesa-Kathā, 13. Gandhavaṃsa, 14. Sāsanavaṃsa and 15. Sangītivaṃsa.* Here, there is the brief description of all these texts.

The *Dīpavaṃsa* puts together certain well known traditions handed down among the Buddhists of Ceylon. Its authorship is unknown. It was written probably in between the begining of the 4th century and the first-third of the 5th century A.D.

Mahāvaṃsa was written by Mahānāma, who lived in the last quarter of the 5th century A.D. *Dīpavaṃsa* and Mahāvaṃsa show far-reaching aggrements in respect of the subject-matter and the arrangement, and both of them have a number of common verses.

The *Cūlavaṃsa* is not an uniform and homogenous work. It is a series of additions to, continuations of the *Mahāvaṃsa.*

The *Buddhaghosuppatti* deals with the life and career of Buddhaghosa, the famous commentator. The book is written in an easy language. It is more or less a historical romance. It was written by a Ceylonese monk named Mahāmangala.

The *Saddhammasaṅgaha* is a work of quasi-historical importance and its interest lies mainly in religious instruction. Though the historical materials are drawn from old Pāli texts, the work has an interest of its own. The book was composed by Dhammakitti Mahāsāmī probably in the 14th century.

---

3 M.Winternitz, *History of Indian Literature*, Vol.II, Bharatiya Vidya Prakashan, Delhi, 1987, p.192.

The *Sandesa-kathā*, written mostly in prose, dilates on many points, e.g. the composition of *Abhidhammatthasaṅgaha* by Thera Aruruddha, the composition of a commentory known as the *Abhidhammattha-vibhāvanī* by Thera Sumangala-Sāmī, etc. It refers to many kingdoms.

The *Mahābodhivaṃsa* or *Bodhivaṃsa* is a prose work, in which Gāthās occur only at the end of the chapters and towards the end of the complete work. It was written by a monk Upatissa in about the end of the 10th century A.D.

The *Thūpavaṃsa* contains an account of the *thūpas* or dagobas built over the relics of the Buddha. It was written by Vācissara, who was teacher of a Ceylonese monk Sangharāja Sāriputta. It was composed in the begining of 12th century A.D.

The *Attanagaluvihāravaṃsa* or *Hatthavanagall-avihāravaṃsa* was written in the thirteenth century A.D. In this book, there is the description of moral character of Ceylonese king Sri Sanghabodhi.

The *Dāṭhāvaṃsa* or *Dantadhātuvaṃsa* is an epic in five cantos composed in Sanskritised Pali (with long compounds) by Monk Dhammakitti in the begining of the 13th century A.D. It is a quasi-religious historical record written with the intention of edifying and at the same time giving an interesting story of the past.

The *Chakesadhātuvaṃsa* is a work by a modern Burmese author of unknown date. It is a mixture of prose and poetry. The language is simple and the diction is noteworthy. It contains an account of the thūpas raised by Sakka, Pajjunna, Maṇinekhalā, Addhikanāvika, Varuṇarāgarāja and Sattanāvika over the heir relics of the Buddha.

The *Nalāṭadhātuvaṃsa* gives the description of the history of bones of forehead of Lord Buddha in five chapters. Although, Geiger considers this text as the composition of 19th century A.D. but there is no real knowledge of its author and period.

We will discuss about the text *Gandhavaṃsa* seperately. The *Sāsanavaṃsa* was written in Burma by Bhikkhu Paññāsāmī in the year 1861. This book gives an account of the growth and expansion of Buddhism. The whole text is written in prose except for a few verses here and there.

The *Saṃgītivaṃsa* was composed by a Thai monk named Somadeja Vanaratana in The year 1789. In it, there is the description of nine Buddhist councils.

B. GANDHAVAṂSA

The *Gandhavaṃsa,* which is a non-cononical Pali work of a later dạte, is a recognised work of traditional history of Pali literature. It discusses the history of Buddhist canons. It also contains a brief history of modern Pali works, which is more detailed than that of *Sāsanavaṃsa.*

The colophon of the text *Gandhavaṃsa* mentions that this was composed by a forest dwelling Elder named Nandapaññā, a learned one, who was born at Hansāraṭṭha and endowed with virtue and energy. The text says that -

> *"So hansāraṭṭhajāto Nandapañño, ti visuto,*
> *Saddhāsīlaviriyupeto dhammasāragavesano. So yaṃ.*
> *Santi sabhāvaṃ nibbānaṃ gavesanto punappunaṃ,*
> *vasento taṃ manorommaṃ piṭakattayasaṅgaha,*
> *Gandhavaṃsaṃ imaṃ khuddaṃ nissāya jaṅghadāsakaṃ'ti.*
> *Iti pāmojjatthāyāraññavāsinā nandapaññācariyena kato cullagandhavaṃso niṭṭhito."*[4]

Minayeff, the editor of *Gandhavaṃsa* in Roman script, after having compared with *Sāsanavaṃsa* and *Piṭakatthamain*, had concluded that *Gandhavaṃsa* is the composition of 17th century A.D. This statement had also been supported by M.Bode.[5] But W. Geiger has kept this text under Pali literature of 19th century A.D.[6] Bhikshu Dharmarakkhita also says that the *Gandhavaṃsa* is the composition of 19th century A.D.[7] Bharat Singh Upadhyaya says that the *Gandhavaṃsa* must be a composition after 17th century A.D., because in the

---

4 G.V., p.35.
5 Bode, M.H., *Pali Literature of Burma*, p.10.
6 W. Geiger, *Pali Literature and Language*, p.48.
7 Bhikshu Dharmarakkhita, *Pāli Sāhitya kā Itihāsa*, p.191.

Gandhavaṃsa, there is the mention of a Pali poetic text named *Kāyaviratigāthā*, which was composed in the 17th century A.D.[8]

The whole text is written in prose except for a few verses here and there. The style is mainly based upon that of Buddhaghosa and his successors. But, the author has not been able to bring out that lucid and placid style, which is manifested in the *Aṭṭhakathas*. The text sometimes remains rather weak in expression and inferior in style. But, its elegant and simple language is charming. The text calls itself *Cullagandhavaṃsa* (short history of books), in the end of each chapter. Possibly, there existed also one *Mahāgandhavaṃsa*. In other words, it can be assumed that present form of *Gandhavaṃsa* is an abridged edition of larger work.

For knowing the history of Pāli books treasure, this text *Gandhavaṃsa* is very useful. In it, there are some big mistakes and also new informations. This text is unfortunately very sparing of details and gives us little information as to the period of the works, it enumerates, but its help is most useful in settling some questions of authorship and place. For the students of Pali literature, the study of this book is very necessary.

The text has been divided into five chapters. The summary of all the five chapters is as follows : -

CHAPTER I

The text opens with salutation to the Buddha in verse and next follows a description of Canon according to *Piṭaka, Nikāya, Aṅga* and *Dhammakkhandha*. All the teachings of Buddha have been classified from different standpoints. These divisions are briefly described in the following manners :-

ONE FOLD DIVISION

All the teachings of the Buddha has only one essence viz., the essence of emancipation. It has been said in the text - "*Sabbaṃ pi buddhavacanaṃ vimuttirasahetukaṃ*".[9] The Bud-

8 Bharat Singh Upadhyaya, *Pāli sāhitya kā Itihāsa*, pp.695-96.

dha himself clarified this by giving the simili of ocean water. He said that - as the great ocean has got only one taste, i.e. salty, similarly my entire teachings has got only one taste, i.e. the tase of emanicipation - *"Seyyathāpi, bhikkhave, mahāsamuddo ekaraso loṇaraso, evameva kho, bhikkhave, ayaṃ dhammavinayo ekaraso vimuttiraso."*[10]

THREE FOLD DIVISION

The most important among the different classification of *Buddhavacana* is form the standpoint of *Piṭakas* in which the words of the Master were classified, according to the subject matter. The general meaning of *Piṭaka* is 'basket, but here in this context, the term *Piṭaka* connotes a technical meaning *pariyatti* - "*pariyatti pi hi mā piṭakasampadānenā*".[11] Here, *pariyatti* denotes the teachings of Buddha and the basket which contained these teachings were called as *piṭaka*. Buddhaghosa has also mentioned this as -

"Piṭakaṃ piṭakatthavidu pariyattibhājanatthato āhu,
Tena samodhānetvā tayo pi vinayādayo ñeyyā."[12]

In Buddhist tradition, we find this division of *Piṭaka* was confined in three *Piṭakas* namely *Vinaya Piṭaka, Abhidhamma Piṭaka* and *Sutta Piṭaka*. The *Gandhavaṃsa* also says that -

"kathaṃ piṭakato ? Piṭakaṃ hi tividhaṃ hoti. Vinaya pitakaṃ, abhidhammapiṭakaṃ suttantapiṭakaṃ ti."[13]

All the teachings, related to monastic life and expressed in the form of norms to regulate the life of monks and nuns, were put in one division, i.e. *Vinaya Piṭaka*. The teachings of *Vinaya Piṭaka* has been termed as '*adhisheel*' teaching - "*Tathā hi vinayapiṭake visesena adhisīlasikkhā vuttā.*"[14] Ācārya Buddhaghosa has defined the *Vinaya Piṭaka* as -

"vividhavisesanayattā vinayato ceva kāyavācanaṃ,
vinayatthaviduhi ayaṃ vinayo vinayo ti akkhāto."[15]

---

9 G.V., p.1.
10 K.N.I. p.128.
11 A.N.I, p.189.
12 Asl., p.18.
13 G.V., p.1.
14 Asl., p.19.

The *Vinaya Piṭaka* has been divided into three parts - (1) *Suttavibhaṅga* (2) *Khandhaka* and (3) *Parivāra*. Again, the *Suttavibhaṅga* has been sub divided into two parts i.e. *Pārājikā* and *Pācittiya*. According to another standpoint, these two sub divisions are called as *Bhikkhu Pātimokkha and Bhikkhunī Pātimokkha*. *Khandhaka* consists of two parts viz., *Mahāvagga* and *Cullavagga*. *Parivāra* consists of all the residual teachings of the aforesaid division. Nandapaññā says that -

> "*Pārājikakaṇḍaṃ, pācittiyakaṇḍaṃ, mahāvagg-akaṇḍaṃ, cullavaggakaṇḍaṃ, parivārakaṇḍaṃ ti imāni kaṇḍāni vinayapiṭakaṃ nāma.*"[16]

Again, *Vinaya Piṭaka* has been explained with three attributes like - (a) teachings related to prescriptions to do this and not to do this *(āṇā-desanā)*, (b) the regulations prescribing punishments according to transgressions (*yathāparādha-sāsana*) and (c) norms of putting restrains over psycho-physio-vocal deeds, indicating the situations, where to put and where *not to put (saṃvara-asaṃvara kathā).*[17]

The second division of the *Buddhavacana* according to the *Piṭakas* is called *Abhidhamma-Piṭaka*. This *Piṭaka* includes the sermons which were profoundly excellent, preponderant and dealing mainly with ultimate realities. It is described as excellent dhamma (*dhammātireka*) and distinguished dhamma (*dhamma-visesa*).[18] It exceeds and is distinguished from the teachings of the *Vinaya* and *Sutta*, both in style and contents. It has also been called as *Paramattha-desanā*.[19] Ācarya Buddhaghosa, while enumerating its special qualities, has said a *gāthā*-

> "*Yaṃ ettha buḍhimanto salakkhaṇā pujitā paricchinnā.*
> *vuttādhikā ca dhammā abhidhammo tena akkhāto.*"[20]

---

15 Asl., p.16.
16 G.V., p.1.
17 Asl., p.18.
18 "*Dhammātireka-dhammavisesa-atthena abhidhammo*"- Asl., p.1.
19 "*Abhidhammapiṭakaṃ paramatthakusalena bhagavatā paramattha-bāhullato desitattā paramatthadesanā'ti vuccati* - S.V.I., p.26.
20 Asl., p.17.

Three atributes are also seen to highlight the nature of *Abhidhamma* as - (1) The teachings related to ultimate truth (*paramattha desanā*) (2) treatment of dhammas as they really are (*yathā-dhamma-sāsana*) and (3) the discourse related to minute analysis of mind and matter (*nāma-rūpa-pariccheda-kathā*).[21]

There are seven books of *Abhidhamma Piṭaka* namely, (i) *Dhammasaṅgaṇi,* (ii) *Vibhaṅga*, (iii) *Dhātukathā,* (iv) *Puggalapaññatti,* (v) *Kathāvatthu* (vi) *Yamaka* and (vii) *Paṭṭhāna*. The *Gandhavaṃsa* also says that -

> *"Dhammasaṅgaṇi-pakaraṇaṃ, vibhaṅga-pakaraṇaṃ, dhātukathā-pakaraṇaṃ, paññatti-pakaraṇaṃ, kathāvatthu-pakaraṇaṃ, yamaka-pakaraṇaṃ, paṭṭhāna-pakaranaṃ, imāni satta pakaraṇāni abhidhammapiṭakaṃ nāma".*[22]

The teachings of the Buddha, which were given with full consideration to the temperament, mental faculties and beliefs of the people, were put into *Sutta-Piṭaka*. The collection of these practical sermons in this *piṭaka* has been due to some certain reasons, which is as follows -

> *"Atthānaṃ sucanato suvuttato savanato ' tha sudanato, suttāṇā suttasabhāgato ca suttaṃ suttaṃ ti akkhātaṃ."*[23]

The *Sutta Piṭaka* has also been described similarly with three attributes as its being the popular discourses *(vohāra desanā)*, teaching given according to the temperament and the elevation of mind (*yathānuloma-sāsana*) and the discourses related to the removal of wrong views (*diṭṭhiviniveṭṭhana-kathā*).[24] The factors, which make the mind fickle, as also those which make them stable and help in concentration, have been elaborately discussed in the discourses and such the teachings of this *piṭaka* has been called *adhicittasikkhā*, the right adherence to which, helps in ficklemindlessness.[25]

There are five parts of *Sutta Piṭaka* namely, *Dīghanikāya*,

---

21 Ibid.
22 G.V., p.2.
23 Asl., p.17.
24 Ibid., p.18.
25 "*Suttantapiṭake adhicittasikkhā*" - Ibid., p.19.

Majjhimanikāya, *Saṃyuttanikāya*, *Aṅguttaranikāya* and *Khuddakanikāya*. The *Gandhavaṃsa* says -- "*Sīlakkhandhavaggādikaṃ avasesaṃ buddhavacanaṃ suttantapiṭakaṃ nāmā.*[26]

In this way, the division of *Buddha-vacana* from the point of *Piṭaka* is called three fold.

FIVE FOLD DIVISION

This is a very important division of the *Buddhavacana*, where the division was done on the basis of *Nikāyas*. The literal meaning of the word '*Nikāya*' is group, division or class but in the Buddhist tradition, this term denotes group and division both. Ācarya Buddhaghosa has defined this word as - *samuha nivāsā hi nikāyo ti pavuccanti.*[27]

To prove this, Buddhaghosa has given examples, e.g. "*Nāhaṃ bhikkhave aññaṃ ekanikāyaṃ pi samanupassāmi evaṃ cittaṃ yathayidaṃ bhikkhave tiracchānagatā pāṇā, poṇikanikāyo, cikkhillikanikāyo"ti.*[28] Here, the word *ekanikāyaṃ* denotes the sense of group. However, in the second example, in which he has referred to the words '*poṇikanikāyo*' *or cikkhillinikāyo,* the word *nikāya* denotes the sense of position (*place*).

From the view point of *nikāya,* the entire *Buddhavacana* has been rendered into five parts, namely (i) *Dīghanikāya*, (ii) *Majjhimanikāya*, (iii) *Saṃyuttanikāya*, (iv) *Aṅguttaranikāya* and (v) *Khuddakanikāya.*[29]

(i)*Dīghanikāya* - The word *dīgha* means 'long'. Here, the long discourses of Buddha were grouped together which had been seperated into three classes namely (i) *Sīlakkhandha-vagga*, (ii) *Mahāvagga* and (iii) *Pātheya* or *Pāthikavagga*, each comprising of thirteen, ten and eleven sūtras respectively.[30]

---

26 G.V., p.2.
27 Asl., p.22.
28 Asl., p.22.
29 "*Dīghanikāyo majjihimanikāyo samuttanikāyo aṅguttaranikāyo khuddakanikāyo ti*" - G.V., p.2.
30 "*Tattha katamo Dīghanikāyo? Sīlakkhandhavaggo mahāvaggo pādhiyavaggo/ ti ime tayo vaggā dīghanikāyo*

Here, a question arises that why this division was termed as *Dīghanikāya*?

In respect of this question, Buddhaghosa has justified by saying that this nomenclature was coined due to the collection of all those sūtras which were lengthy in group and place - "*dīghappamāṇānaṃ suttānaṃ samuhato ca nivāsato ca.*"[31]

However, this explanation did not justify the question fully for, if the length of the sutras were to be the main criterion then, we find also some sutras which are by no means longer than the ones which are included in *Majjhimanikāya.*[32] For example, quantitavely the length of *Dīghanikāya's Jāliyasutta*, *Mahāsamayasutta* and that of *Nivāpasutta* and *Vammikasutta* of *Majjhimanikāya* are almost similar. So, the most plausible explanation of the name *Dīgha* is that the largest collection of the lengthy sayings have been grouped under this *nikāya*.

(ii) *Majjhimanikāya* - The second division according to the Nikāya's classification is *Majjhimanikāya*. The discourses which were of medium length were placed under the *Majjhimanikāya.*[33] There were one hundred fifty two suttas which were divided into three main divisions namely *Mūlapaṇṇāsa*, *Majjhimapaṇṇāsa* and *Uparipaṇṇāsa*.

The *Gandhavaṃsa* also says that -

"*Mūlapaṇṇāso majjhimapaṇṇāso uparipaṇṇāso ti ime tayo paṇṇāsā majjhimanikāyo nāma. Imesu tīsu paṇṇāsesu dve paṇṇāsadhikasuttasatāni honti. Dviyaḍḍhasatasuttantā dvisuttaṃ yassa santi so, Majjihimanikāyo nāma mūlapaṇṇāsa-ādiko'ti.*"[34]

(iii) *Saṃyuttanikāya* - The literal meaning of '*saṃyutta*' is mixed. The mixed type of discourses, i.e. some long and some short and also some of the medium length were put

---

nāma. Imesu tīsu vaggesu catutinsa suttāni ca honti."-Ibid.

31 Asl., p.22.

32 D.N.I., pp. 136-37; II, pp. 189-196; M.N.I, pp. 188-91.

33 "*Majjhimappamāṇāni pañcadasa - vaggasaṅgahāni mūlapariyāya-suttādīni dviyaḍḍhasataṃ dve ca suttāni*" - Asl., p.22.

34 G.V., p.2.

together in this *nikāya*. There were seven thousand seven hundred and sixty-two discourses in all which were divided in five classes viz. *Sagāthavagga, Nidānavagga, Khandhavagga, Salāyatanavagga* and *Mahāvagga*. Again each of three *vaggas* had been divided into *saṃyuttas*, which contain numerous suttas. In total, there were fifty-six *saṃyuttas* in the five vaggas. The text *Gandhavaṃsa* says - "*Sagāthāvaggo nidānavaggo salāyatanavaggo khandhakavaggo mahāvaggo'ti ime panca vaggā saṃyuttanikāyo nāma. Imesu pañcasu vaggesu dvāsaṭṭhi sattasatādhikasattasuttasahassāni honti.*

Dvasaṭṭhisasttasattāni sasttasahassakāni ca,
Suttāni yassa honti sagāthādikavaggiko,
Saṃyuttanikāyo nāma viditabbo viññūnā' ti."[35]

In *Saṃyuttanikāya*, discourses are both in verses as well as in *gāthās*.

(iv) *Aṅguttaranikāya* - This is the fourth collection of *Buddha-vacana* according to the *Nikāya* point of view. Here, the sermons were collected in the ascending numerical order. The suttas, some nine thousand five hundred fifty seven,[36] are arranged in one hundred sixty vaggas in eleven section from one to eleven. Each section has been arranged in such a manner that section one treats of things, which are only one in number while section two of things which are two in number and so on.[37] The text *Gandhavaṃsa says* -

"*Ekkanipāto dukkanipāto tikkanipāto catukkanipāto pañcanipāto chakkanipāto sattanipāto aṭṭhanipāto navanipāto dasanipāto ekādasanipāto' ti ime ekādasa nipātā aṅguttaranikāyo nāma. Imesu ekādasasu nipātesu sattapaṇṇāsa pañcasatādhikanavasuttasahassāni honti.*
Navasuttasahassāni pañcasatāni ca,
Sattapaṇṇāsādhikāni suttāni yassa honti.
So aṅguttaranikāyo'ti' ekanipātādiko'ti."[38]

(v) *Khuddakanikāya* - *Khuddaka* means small. It is considered as the fifth *Nikāya*, the subject matter of which

---

35 G.V, p.3.
36 "*Navasuttasahassāni pañca suttasatāni ca.*
Sattapaññāsasuttāni saṅkhā aṅguttare ayaṃ"*-Asl., p.22*
37 Ibid.
38 G.V., p.3.

contains the entire *Vinaya Piṭaka*, whole *Abhidhamma Piṭaka* and fifteen books like *Khuddakapāṭha, Dhammapada, Udāna, Itivuttaka, Suttanipāta, Vimānavatthu, Petavatthu, Theragāthā, Therīgāthā, Jātaka, Niddesa, Paṭisambhidāmagga, Avadāna, Buddhavaṃsa* and *Cariyāpiṭaka.* It is said - "*sakalaṃ vinayapiṭakaṃ, abhidhammapiṭakaṃ, khuddakapāṭha, dhammapadādayo ca pubbe dassitā pañcadasappabhedā; ṭhapetvā cattāro nikāye avasesaṃ Buddhavacanaṃ ti*"[39]

However, the name *khuddakanikāya* sounds quite unjustified and more so when it also does include both *Vinaya* and *Abhidhamma Piṭaka*. Probably, the compilers of this *nikāya* gave this name *khuddaka* by incorporating into the smaller fifteen books like *khuddakapāṭha* etc. This view is corroborated by Buddhaghosa -

> "*Thapetvā caturo pete nikāye dīgha-ādike.*
> *Tadaññaṃ buddhavacanaṃ nikāyo khuddako mato ti.*"[40]

The text *Gandhavaṃsa* also says that -

> "*Anekāni suttasahassāni niddiṭṭhāni mahesinā.*
> *Nikāye pañcame ramme khuddako'ti visuto'.*"[41]

In this way the entire *Buddhavacana* has been divided from the standpoint of *Nikāya* in five-folds.

NINE FOLD DIVISION

The words of the Buddha is also divided into nine ways on the basis of *aṅgas* (types). In this system of division all the words of the Buddha are classified into nine types viz. (i) sutta, (ii) *Geyya,* (iii) *Veyyākaraṇa*, (iv) *Gāthā,* (v) *Udāna,* (vi) *Itivuttaka*, (vii) *Jātaka*, (viii) *Abbhutadhamma* and (ix) *Vedalla*[42]. Here, there is the brief description of all these nine types.

(i) *Sutta* - Though Buddha's each and every teaching is known as *sutta* or *sūtra,* but here this word has been used in a specifie way. Here, it includes the *Bhikkhu-vibhaṅga*, the

---

39 Asl., p.22.
40 Asl., p.22
41 G.V., p.3.
42 G.V., p.3.

Bhikkhunī-Vibhaṅga, *Niddesa*, *Khandhakas*, *Parivāra* as well as the *Maṅgalasutta*, *Ratanasutta* etc.[43]

(ii) *Geyya* - All the verses, which can be recited just like a song are called *'Geyya'*. "*sabbaṃ pi sagāthakaṃ geyyaṃ ti veditabbaṃ 'ti'*." In particular, all the chapters with verses in the *saṃyuttanikāya* form *Geyya*.

(iii) *Veyyākaraṇa* - The entire *Abhidhamma Piṭaka*, suttas without verses and other words of the Buddha, which are not included in the eight types are included in *Veyyākaraṇa* (Skt. Vyākaraṇa) or exposition.[44]

However, the *vyākaraṇa* includes only those sutras which are devoid of verses.[45] Moreover, the *vyākaraṇa* has further been defined as "*vyākriyante sabdā aneneti saddānajānakaṃ vyākaraṇam,*" which also is in conformity by the definition provided in the Laghu Siddhānta Kaumudi.[46]

(iv) *Gāthā* - The *Dhammapada*, the *Theragathā,* the *Therīgāthā,* those pieces of the *Suttanipāta*, which are not called suttas and which are entirely in verse are included in *Gāthā*.[47]

(v) *Udāna* - *Udāna* means pithy sayings and were those which were uttered by the Buddha out of immense joy. According to *Gandhavaṃsa*, *Udāna* comprises of eighty - two *suttantas* coupled with verses, expressive of religious emotions.[48] Although Ācārya Buddhaghosa have defined *udāna* as

---

43 "*Tattha ubhatovibhaṅganiddese khandhakaparivārā suttanipāte maṅgalasuttaṃ ratanasuttaṃ nālakasutta tuvaṭṭakasutta aññaṃ pi suttanāmakaṃ tathāgatavacanaṃ suttaṃ ti veditabbaṃ*" - G.V. pp.3-4.

44 "*Sakalaṃ abhidhammapiṭakaṃ nigāthakaṃ suttaṃ ca. yaṃ ca aññaṃ pi aṭṭhahi aṅgehi asaṃgahitaṃ buddhavacanaṃ taṃ buddhavacanaṃ veyyākaraṇaṃ veditabbaṃ*" - G.V., pp. 3-4 ·

45 "*Vyākaranameva veyākaraṇam' ti*" - *Nettipakarana - aṭṭhakthā*, p.13

46 "*Dhammapada - Theragāthā - Therīgāthā Suttanipāte nosutta - nāmikā suddhikagāthā ca gāthā'ti veditabbā*" - G.V., p.4.

47 "*Somanassañānamayikagāthā paṭisamyuttā dve asītisuttantā udānaṃ'ti veditabbaṃ'ti*" - Ibid.

only those sentences which were coupled with the joyful utterances by Buddha in the form of *Gāthā*.

(vi) *Itivuttaka* - In this type, all the discourses start with the word - 'Thus it was said by the Blessed one" (*vuttaṃ hetaṃ Bhagavatā). In end of each sutta either - ayaṃ pi attho vutto Bhagavatā* or "*iti me suttaṃ ti*" is universally found. According to *Gandhavaṃsa*, out of the whole *Buddhavacana*, only one hundred and twelve suttas can be atributed to *Itivuttaka.*[49]

(vii) *Jātaka* - It comprises of around five hundred fifty tales of previous births of Buddha.[50] All of these tales are connected with the activities of the Bodhisattva prior to his achievement of Bodhi. However, in Pali tradition, there are only five hundred fourty seven tales are extant.[51]

(viii) *Abbutadhamma* - This is also a type of the division of *Buddhavacana.* It comprises those suttas which explain some wonderous activities of Buddha and through which exclamatory detailes are found.[52] It has been defined so far, when Buddha gave discourses on Dhamma, it was listened to by all those persons, who were completely involved in the mundane affairs of the life. Far from being indifferent to those utterences, these people liked them and started treading upon that fruitful path which Lord Buddha showed them for their benefit. This happening was quite wonderful and unbelievable.

(ix) *Vedalla* - It comprises such discourses which are in the form of questions asked through repeated attainment of delight and understanding. The suttas which mainly are included in *Vedalla* are *Cullavedalla sutta, Mahāvedalla sutta, Sammādiṭṭhi, Saṅkhārabhājaniya, Sakkapañhā* etc.[53]

---

48 "*Somanassañānamayikagāthāpaṭisamyuttā dve asītisuttantā udānaṃ'ti veditabbaṃ'ti* - G.V., p.4.

49 "*Vuttaṃ hetaṃ bhagavatā'ti ādinayapavatto dvādasuttarasatasuttantā itivuttakaṃ' ti veditabbā*" - G.V. p.4 ; Asl., p.22.

50 "*Apaṇṇakajātakādīni paṇṇāsādhikāni pañcajātakasatāni jātakaṃ ti veditabbā* " - Ibid.

51 Bharat Singh Upadhyaya, *Pali sāhitya kā Itihāsa, pp. 297-300.*

52 "*Acchariya-abbutadhammapaṭisamyuttā suttantā abbhuta-dhammaṃ'ti veditabbaṃ" - G.V.,p.4; Asl.,* p.23.

EIGHTY-FOUR THOUSAND FOLD DIVISION

This mammoth division of the *Buddha-vacana* was made from the standpoint of *Dhammakkhandha*, i.e. each *khandha* forms one unit of the words of the Master e.g. a question put by a monk is one *dhammakkhandha* and the answer thereof given by the Buddha is another *dhammakkhandha*.[54]

Ānanda said in the first council that he received eighty two thousand *dhammakkhandha* from the Buddha and two thousand form the Bhikkhu Sāriputta. As such, in total, there were eighty-four thousand unit of *Dhammakkhandha*,[55] which was a sum total of twenty-one thousand units of *Vinaya-piṭaka*, another twenty one thousand units of *Sutta-piṭaka* and the remaining forty-two thousand of *Abhidhamma-piṭaka*.

This has been elaborated further that the suttas containing one theme forms one unit of text. The suttas containing more than one unit of text, and in such cases, unit of texts were determined by the numbr of such themes.[56] In the *Abhidhamma*, each tribal (*tika*) or dual (*duka)* classification, as well as each classification of conscious intervals , forms one unit of text.[57] In the *Vinaya*, there are subject, offence, regarding the rules of conduct, tables of contents, classification of terms, interim offence, innocence and division into triplets which are understood as an individual unit of text.[58]

---

53 "*Cullavedalla - mahāvedalla - sammādiṭṭhi - sakkapañhā-saṃkhārabhājanīyamahāpuṇṇa - mahāsuttantādayo sabbe pi vedaṃ ca tuṭṭhiṃ ca laddhāladdhā - pucchitasuttantā vedallaṃ'ti veditabbaṃ* - Ibid.

54 "*Ekaṃ vatthuṃ eko dhammakkhandh, ekaṃ nidānaṃ eko dhammakkhandho, ekaṃ pañhāpucchanaṃ eko dhammakkhandho ekaṃ pañhāvisajjanaṃ eko dhammakkhandho*" - G.V., p.4.

55 "*Dvāsītiṃ buddhato gaṇhiṃ dve sahassāni bhikkhuto, caturāsīti sahassāni ye' me dhammā pavattino ti* -" Asl., p.23.

56 "*Ekānusandhikaṃ suttaṃ eko dhammakkhandho. Yaṃ anekānusadhikaṃ tattha anusandhivasena dhammakkhandhagaṇanā* - Ibid.

57 "*Abhidhamme ekamekaṃ tikadukabhājanaṃ ekamekaṃ ca cittavārabhājanaṃ eko dhammakkhandho* " - Ibid.

In this way the entire *Buddhavacana* was divided into eighty four thousand fold.

CHAPTER II

The second chapter deals with the authors of the books. The authors have been divided into the classes, which is also in a chronological sequence. The three classes are namely (i) *Parāṇācariya* (ii) *Aṭṭhakathācariya* and (iii) *Gandhakācariya*.

According to Nandapaññā, the five hundred Arhants, who named the five nikāyas, made their meaning and purports, their exposition and correction in the First council as well as the seven hundred Arhants, who made their proper interpretation, etc. in the second council, together with one thousand Arhats, who also made their proper interpretation in the Third council, are known as the *Porāṇācariya* except Mahākaccāyana.[59] Again, it is distinctly stated in the *Gandhavaṃsa* that those who are the *Porāṇācariyā* are also the *Aṭṭhakathācariya*, or the teachers who wrote the Aṭṭhakathas.[60] Buddhaghosa speaks of the *porāṇā* or *Porāṇakatthera*[61] as persons, who declare that those who observe the precepts, will uphold the Buddhasāsana or the teachings of the Lord. It is said in connection with those, who

---

58 "*Vinaye atthi vatthu, atthi mātikā, atthi padabhājaniyaṃ, atthi āpatti, atthi anāpatti, atthi antarāpatti, atthi tikacchedo. Tattha ekameko koṭṭhāso ekameko dhammakkhendho ti veditabbo*" - Ibid.

59 "*Paṭhama-saṅgāyanāyaṃ pañca satā khiṇāsavā, pañcannaṃ nikāyānaṃ nāmaṃ ca atthaṃ ca, adhippāyaṃ ca padaṃ ca, byañjanaṃ ca, sodhanakiccaṃ anavasesaṃ karinsu. Dutiya-sangāyanāyaṃ satta satā khiṇāsavā tesaṃ yeva saddatthādikaṃ kiccaṃ puna karinsu. Tatiya-saṅgāyanāyaṃ sahassamattā khiṇāsavā tesaṃ yeva saddatthādikaṃ kiccaṃ puna karinsu. Iccevaṃ dve sattādhikā dvesahassakhīṇāsavā mahākaccāyanaṃ ṭhapetvā avasesā porāṇācariyā nāma*" - G.V., p.6.

60 "*ye porāṇācariyā te yeva aṭṭhakathācariyā nāma* " - Ibid.

61 "*Teneva porāṇakatthera : lajji rakkhissati, lajji rakkhissatīti tikkhattuṃ āhaṃsu* " - *Visuddhimagga*, p.99 (PTS)

learn Dhamma from their teachers and maintain the views of their teachers. They don't entertain any dogmatic view of their own. Some traditional sayings of legendary or doctrinal character are cited by Buddhaghosa, in the name of *Porāṇa*. Mrs. Rhys Davids suggests that these *Porānas* represented on evolving school of philosophical thought.[62] B.C. law considers that the name refers to eminent and revered teachers of the order, who were often asked to interpret question arising among the saṃgha and whose interpretations were embodied in the Great *Aṭṭhakathas* ; and he suggests that these were preserved in the Great Sinhalese commentaries and distinguished by being quoted in the original Pali.[63] G.P. Malalsekera[64] is of the opinion that the *Poraṇās* merely refer to teachers, whose expositions were not necessarily embodied in the commentaries, but handed down in the various schools by oral tradition, sometimes with mnemonic verses to help the memory and that Buddhaghosa refers to such traditional explanations as the anonymous *Porāṇa*. Often in Sinhalese books, when the author quoting from an ancient work either, does not know - or does not think it necessary to give - the source, he introduces it merely by - '*eheyim purātaṇayo kīhu*' ('therefore the ancients said').

Gandhakārakācariyas were those persons who composed the commentaries. Among *Gandhakārakācariyas*, there were firstly the authors of Kurundi and Mahāpaccari etc. sinhalese commentaries and then Buddhaghosa, Buddhadutta, Ānanda and Dhammapāla wrote the commentaries on the different texts.

After having introduced these three teachers, the author proceeds to the works of different teachers namely Mahāvajirabuddhi, Vimalabuddhi, Cullavajira, Dīpaṅkara etc. In it, there is the description of fifty six authors, one hundred forty eight books and thirty books, written by unknown writers. In total, there is the description of one hundred seventy eight

---

62 Law, B.C., *The life and work of Buddhaghosa*, (Foreword), Calcutta, 1923, p.vii.

63 Ibid., p.64

64 Malalsekera, G.P., *The Pali Literature of Ceylon*, Colombo, 1958, p.92.

books. Under it, the books of *Tipiṭaka* are not included and the book *Milindapañha* has not been mentioned. A list of authors and their-works as stated in the *Gandhavaṁsa* is given below :-

1. Mahākaccāyana :- Kaccāyanagandho, Mahāniruttigandho, Cullaniruttigandho, Nettigandho, Peṭakopadesagandho, Vaṇṇanītigandho.
2. Buddhaghosa :- Visuddhimaggo, Sumaṅgalavilāsinī, Papañcasūdanī, Sāratthāpakāsinī, Manorathapūraṇī, Samantapāsādikā, Paramatthakathā, Kaṅkhāvitaraṇī, Dhammapadaṭṭhakathā, Jātakaṭṭhakathā, Khuddakapāṭhaṭṭhakathā, Apadānaṭṭhakathā.
3. Buddhadutta :- Vinayavinicchayo, Uttaravinicchayo, Abhidhammāvatāro, Madhuratthavilāsinī.
4. Ānanda : - Mūlaṭīkaṁ.
5. Dhammapāla :- Nettipakaraṇaṭṭhakathā, Itivuttaka-aṭṭhakathā, Udānaṭṭhakathā, Cariyāpiṭaka-aṭhakathā, Theragāthāṭṭhakathā, Vimānavatthussa Vimalavilāsinī nāma aṭṭhakathā, Petavatthussa Vimalavilāsinī nāma aṭṭhakathā, Paramatthamañjūsā, Dīghanikāyaṭṭhakathādīnaṁ catunnaṁ aṭṭhakathānaṁ Līnatthapakāsinī nāma ṭīkā, Jātakaṭṭhakathāya Līnatthapakāsinī nāma ṭīkā, Paramatthadīpanī, Līnatthavaṇṇanā.
6. Mahāvajirabuddhi : - Vinayagaṇḍhi.
7. Vimalabuddhi :- Mukhamattadīpanī.
8. Cullavajiro :- Atthabyakkhyānaṁ.
9. Dīpaṁkaro :- Rūpasiddhipakaraṇaṁ, Rūpasiddhiṭīkaṁ Summapañcasuttaṁ.
10. Culladhammapālo :- Saccasaṁkhepaṁ.
11. Kassapo :- Mohavicchedanī, Vimaticchedanī, Buddhavaṁsa, Anāgatavaṁsa.
12. Mahānāma :- Saddhammapakāsanī, Mahāvaṁsa, Cullavaṁsaṁ.
13. Upasena :-Saddhammaṭṭhitikaṁ.
14. Moggallāna :- Moggallānabyākaraṇaṁ.
15. Saṁgharakkhita :- Subodhālaṁkāraṁ.
16. Vuttodayakāra :- Vuttodaya, Saṁbandhacintā, Navaṭīkaṁ.
17. Dhammasiri :- Khuddasikkhaṁ.

18. Anuruddha :- Khuddasikkhaṃ.
19. Anurddha :- Paramatthavinicchayaṁ, Nāmarūparicchedaṁ, Abhidhammatthasaṁgahapakaranaṁ.
20. Khema :- Khemaṁ.
21. Sāriputta :- Sāratthadīpanī, Vinayasaṁgahapakaraṇaṁ, Sāratthamaṇjūsaṁ, Pañcakaṁ.
22. Buddhanāga :- Vinayatthamañjūsaṁ.
23. Navo Moggallāna :- Abhidhānappadīpikaṁ.
24. Vācissaro :- Sambandhacintāṭikā, Moggallānabyākaraṇassaṭikā, Nāmarūparicchedaṭīkā, Padarūpavibhāvaṇam, Khemapakaraṇassaṭīkā, Mūlasikkhāyaṭīkā, Vuttodayavivaranaṁ, Sumaṅgalapasādanī, Bālāvatāro, Yogavinicchayo, Sīmālaṅkāra, Rūpārūpavibhāga, Paccayasaṁgaho.
25. Sumaṅgala :- Abhidhammatthavikāsanī, Abhidhammattha-Vibhāvanī.
26. Dhammakitti :- Dantadhātupakaraṇaṁ.
27. Medhaṁkaro :- Jinacaritaṁ.
28. Saddhammasiri :- Saddatthabhedacintā.
29. Devo :- Sumaṇakūṭavaṇṇanā.
30. Cullabuddhaghoso :- Jātattagīnidānaṁ, Sotattagīnidānaṁ.
31. Raṭṭhapāla :- Madhurasavāhinī.
32. Aggavaṁsa :- Saddanīitipakaraṇaṁ.
33. Vimalabuddhi :- Mahāṭīkaṁ.
34. Uttama :- Bālāvatāraṭīkaṁ, Liṅgatthavivaranaṭīkaṁ.
35. Kyacvārañño :- Saddabindu, Paramatthabindupakaraṇaṁ.
36. Saddhammaguru :- Saddavuttipakāsanaṁ.
37. Aggapaṇḍita :- Lokuppatti.
38. Saddhammajotipāla :- Sīmālaṁkārassaṭīkā. Mātikatthadīpanī, Vinayasamuṭṭhānadīpanī, Gandhasāro, Paṭṭhāngaṇanānayo, Saṁkhepavaṇṇanā, Suttaniddeso, Pātimokkhavisodhanī.
39. Nava Vimalabuddhi : - Abhidhammapaṇṇarasaṭṭhānaṁ.
40. Vepullabuddhi : - Saddasāratthajāliniyāṭīkā, Vuttodayaṭīkā, Paramatthamañjūsā, Dassagaṇḍhivaṇṇanā, Magadhabhūtāvidaggaṁ,

Vidadhimukkhamaṇḍanaṭīkā.

41. Ariyavaṁsa :- Maṇisāramañjūsaṁ, Maṇidīpaṁ, Gaṇḍābharanaṁ, Mahānissaraṁ, Jātakavisodhanaṁ.
42. Cīvaro :- Jaṅghadāsassa ṭīkaṁ.
43. Nava medhaṁkaro :- Lokadīpakasāraṁ.
44. Sāriputto :- Saddavuttipakāsakassaṭīkaṁ.
45. Dhammasenāpati :- Kārikaṁ. Etimāsamidīpakaṁ, and Manohāraṁ.
46. Ñāṇasāgaro :- Liṅgatthavivaraṇapakāsanaṁ.
47. Abhaya :- Saddatthabhedacintāya mahāṭīkaṁ.
48. Guṇasāgaro :- Mukhamattasāraṁ taṭṭīkaṁ.
49. Subhūtacandana :- Liṅgatthavivaraṇapakaraṇaṁ.
50. Udumbaranāmācariyo :- Peṭakopadesassa ṭīkaṁ.
51. Upatissācariya :- Anāgatavaṁsassa aṭṭhakathā.
52. Buddhapiya :- Sāratthasaṁgahanāmagandho.
53. Dhammānandācariya :- Kaccāyanasāro, Kaccāyanabhedaṁ, and Kaccāyanasārassaṭīkā.
54. Gandhācariyo :- Kurundigandha.
55. Nāgītācariya :- Saddasāratthajālinī.

Works of unknown authors mentioned in the *Gandhavaṁsa* are stated below :-

Mahāpaccariyaṁ, Pūrāṇaṭikā, Mūlasikkhāṭikā, Līnatthapakāsinī, Nisandeho, Dhammānusāraṇī, Ñeyyāsandati, Ñeyyāsandatiyā ṭikā, Sumahāvatāro, Lokapaññattipakaraṇaṁ, Tathāgatupattipakaraṇaṁ, Nalāṭadhātuvaṇṇanā, Sīhalavatthu, Dhammadīpako, Paṭipattisaṁgaho, Visuddhimaggagaṇḍhi, Abhidhammagaṇḍhi, Nettipakaraṇagaṇḍhi, Visuddhimagga-cullanavaṭikā, Sotappamālinī, Pasādajananī, Subodhālankārassa Navaṭīkā, Gūlhatthaṭīkaṁ, Bālappabodhanaṁ, Saddatthabhedacintāyamajjhimaṭīkaṁ, Kārikāyaṭikaṁ, Etimāsamidīpikāyaṭikaṁ, Dīpavaṁsa, Thūpavaṃsa, and Bodhivaṃsa.

CHAPTER III

The third chapter throws light on the description of Indian (*Jambudīpakācariya*) and Sinhalese (*Laṅkādīpakācariya*). First of all, there is the description of *Jambudīpakācariyas*. Here, there is the list of the *Jambudīpakācariyas*.

1. Mahākaccāyana
2. Mahābuddhaghosa
3. Buddhadutta
4. Ānanda
5. Dhammapāla

6 & 7. Two pubbācariyas

8. Mahāvajirabuddhi
9. Cullavajirabuddhi
10. Dīpaṃkara
11. Culladhammapāla
12. Kassapa

The author says that Mahākaccāyana, before his conversion, was chaplain to king Canda Pajjota (Paccota) of Ujjeni in the Avanti country.[65] Further, the text mentions that Buddhaghosa was son of the Brahmin Kesi, who was chaplain to king Saṃgāma in the Magadha country.[66]

The below mentioned names are of the Jambudīpakācariyas, who wrote at Arimaddana (Pukkāma) -

1. Subhūtacandana
2. Aggavaṃsa
3. Navavajirabuddhi
4. Vepullabuddhi
5. Gunasāgara
6. Abhaya

---

65 "*Mahākaccāyano jambudīpakācariyo. So hi avantiraṭṭhe ujjenīnagare candapaccotasa nāma rañño purohito hutvā kāmānaṃ ādīnavaṃ disvā gharāvāsaṃ pahāya satthu sāsane pabbajjitvā heṭṭhāvuttapakāre gandhe akāsi* " - G.V., p. 14.

66 "*Mahābuddhaghosācariyo jambudīpako. So kira magadharaṭṭhe saṁgāmarañño purohitassa kesī nāma brahmaṇassa putto satthu sāsane pabbajjitvā laṅkādīpaṃ gato, heṭṭhāvuttappakāre gandhe akāsi* " - Ibid.

7. Ñāṇasāgara
8. Dhammapāla
9 & 10. Another two teachers
11. Uttama
12. Caturangabalamahāmacca
13. Dhammasenāpati
14, 15 & 16. Another three teacher
17. Saddhammaguru
18. Sāriputta
19. Dhammabhinanda
20. Another one teacher
21. Medhaṃkara
22. Aggapaṇḍita
23. Vajira
24. Saddhammapāla
25. Nava Vimalabuddhi

According to the text, there are twenty-three teachers but the list contains twenty-five. In the following passage of the list, the text says that Nava Vimalabuddhi wrote his books at Panyanagara. Ariyavaṃsa and another teacher wrote in Avantipura.[67] Another twenty teachers of Jambudīpa wrote at Kāñcipura (According to the text at Kiñcipura).[68]

After the discription of *Jambudīpakācariyas*, the author makes a list of *Laṅkādīpakācariya*.

1. Mahāaṭṭhakathācariya
2. Mahāpaccarikācariya
3. Mahākurundikācariya

---

67 "*Navo vimalabuddhācariyo jambudīpako heṭṭhāvuttapakāre gandhe panyanagare akaṃsu. Aññatarācariyo ariyavaṃsācariyo'ti ime dvācariyā jambudīpikā heṭṭhāvuttappakāre gandhe avantīpure akaṃsu*"- G.V., p.15.

68 "*Aññatarā vīsatācariyā jambudīpikā heṭṭhāvuttappakāre gandhe kiñcipuranagare akaṃsu* - Ibid.

4 & 5. Two other teachers

6. Mahānāma

7. Another teacher

8. Cullanāma

9. Upasena

10. Moggalāna

11. Sangharakkhita

12. Vācissara

13. Vuttodayakācariya

14. Dhammapāla

15 & 16. Two other teachers

17. Anuruddha

18. Khema

19. Sāriputta

20. Buddhanāga

21. Cullamoggalāna

22. Vācitassapa

23. Sumaṅgala

24. Buddhapiya

25. Dhammakitti

26. Medhṃkara

27. Buddharakkhita

28. Upatissa

29. to 48. Twenty other teachers

49. Saddhammacāra

50. Deva

51. Cullabuddhaghosa

52. Sāriputta

53. Raṭṭhapāla

According to the text, there are fifty one teachers but the list mentions Fifty-three teachers. One Burmese manuscript omits (15) and (16) and another manuscript omits (22). The first five teachers are stated to have lived long before Buddhaghosa.[69]

CHAPTER IV

The fourth chapter discusses about the authors who composed the books either independently or with the request of others. Some of the books were written at the request of teachers and some of the books were written independently or not at the request of teachers. First of all, this chapter starts with the books of Mahākaccāyana. Mahākaccāyana wrote six books independently. Buddhaghosa is the author of thirteen books. Among the works of Buddhaghosa, *Visuddhimagga* was written at the request of Saṅghapāla. According to *Gandhavaṃsa*,[70] the commentary on *Aṅguttara-nikāya* was written at the request of Thera Bhaddanta with an Ājivaka. But, the *Manorathapuraṇi*, says that Buddhaghosa wrote it at the request of Ven. Jotipāla who was staying with him at Kāñcipura.[71]

The commentaries on *Khuddaka-pāṭha* and *Suttanipāta* were written by Buddhaghosa independently.[72]

After that the chapter states about the works of Buddhadutta. Buddhadutta is the author of four books[73] but again the text says that he also composed the text *Jinālaṃkāra* at

69 "*Mahāaṭṭhakathācariyo, mahāpaccarikācariyo, ca mahākurundīkācariyo, aññatarācariyehi ime pañcāriyo lankādīpikācariyo nāma. Te hi buddhaghosācariyassa pure bhūtā cire kāle ahesuṃ*" - G.V.,p.14.

70 "*Aṅguttaranikāyassa aṭṭhakathāgandho bhaddantanāmattherena saha ājīvakena āyācitena buddhaghosācariyana kato* " - G.V., p.17.

71 *Quoted in the 2500 years of Buddhism*, Ed. P.V. Bapat, p.296.

72 "*Khuddakapāṭhassa aṭṭkathāgandho suttanipātassa aṭṭhakathāgandho attano matiyā buddhaghosācariyena katā*" - G.V., p.17.

73 "*Buddhadatto nāmācariyo vinayavinicchayo uttaravinicchayo abhidhammāvatāro buddhavaṃsa madhuratthavilāsini nāma aṭṭhakathā'ti ime cattāro gandhā akāsi* " - G.V., p.7.

the request of Sanghapāla thera.[74]

Ānandācariya wrote Mūlaṭīkā on the *Abhidhamma* at the request of Buddhamitta.

Dhammapāla is the author of fourteen books. The commentaries on *Itivuttaka, Udāna, Cariyāpiṭaka, Theragāthā, Therīgāthā, Vimānavatthu, Petavatthu* and the sub-commentaries of *Dīghanikāya* etc., *Anutikās* on *Abhidhammatthakathā, Jātakaṭṭhakathāṭīkā, Niruttipakaranaṭṭakathāṭīkā, Buddhavamsaṭṭhakathāṭīkā* were written by Dhammapāla independently. And the commentary on *Nettipakaraṇa, Visuddhimagga* were written by Dhammapāla at the request of Dharmarakkhitatthera and Dāṭhānāmatthera respectively.

After that there is the discription of works of other teachers, who composed the books independently and at the request of others.

CHAPTER V

The tenth chapter is mainly devoted to showing the advantages, both mundane and supramundane, of writing the three piṭakas, commentaries etc. It has clearly been stated by the Buddha that after his Mahāparinibbāna, the eighty four thousand *Dhammakkhandhas* will be the Master.[75] These *dhammakkhandhas* have been honoured by him as his *dhammakāya.*[76] At the council of Rājagaha, which was held just after three months of Buddha's emancipation, five hundred Arhats divided these *dhammakkhandhas* into name and section.[77]

Therefore, he, who writes the three Piṭakas, commentaries or causes to be written, is wise and follows the teachings of the Master. Again the text says that whosoever wise and brave man composes the commentary books etc. or causes to compose, his merit accumulation becomes infinite, his

74 "*Jinālaṃkāragandho saṃghapālattherena āyācitena buddhaduttācariyena kato*" - Ibid. p.18.

75 D.N.II, p. 118.

76 S.S., p.45.

77 "*Samgītikāle pañcasatā khiṇāsavā tesaṃ ca dhammakkhandhāṇaṃ nāmavagganipātakā* " - G.V., p.30.

meritorious fruit becomes infinite, like one gets after making eighty-four thousand stupas, like making the image of eighty-four thousand Buddhas, like planting of eighty four thousand Bodhi trees, like making eighty-four thousand monastries.[78] One can get rid of all kinds of sufferings, achieves worldly fame, wealth and prosperity and attains Nibbāna and even the Buddhahood.[79] This account of merit is reminiscent of the analogous records in the *Purāṇas*. Therefore, a wise man, looking for self welfare, may do devotion in the books or may cause to be devoted.[80]

---

78 "*Yo kici paṇḍito vīro aṭṭhakathādikaṃ gandhaṃ karoti kārāpeti vā tassa anantako hoti puññasaṃcayo anantako hoti puññānisamo caturāsīticetiyasahassakaraṇasadiso caturāsītibuddharūpakaraṇasadiso caturāsītibodhirukkha-sahassaropanasadiso caturāsītivihārasahassakaranasadiso* " G.V., p. 30-31.

79 "*Devamanussasampatti anubhoti punappunaṃ, Arahattaphalaṃ patto nibbānaṃ pāpuṇissati* " - Ibid., p.33.

80 "*Tasmā hi paṇḍito poso sampassaṃ hitaṃ attano, kārevvasāmaṃ gandhe ca aññe hi pa kārāpaye*" - Ibid.

नमो तस्स भगवतो अरहतो सम्मासम्बुद्धस्स

गंध-वंसो

पठमो परिच्छेदो

गन्थारम्भ-कथा

R.55 १. नमस्सित्वान सम्बुद्धं, अग्गवंस परम्परं।
नत्वान धम्मं बुद्धजं, संघं चापि निरङ्गणं॥
२. गंधवंसुपनिस्साय, गंधवंसं पकट्टिस्सं।
तिपिटकसमाहारं, साधूनं जंघदासकं।
विमतिनोदं आरब्भं, तं मे सुणाथ साधवो॥
३. सब्बं पि बुद्ध-वचनं, विमुत्तिरस-हेतुकं।
होति एकविधं येव, तिविधं पिटकेन च॥
४. तं च सब्बं पि केवलं, पञ्चविधं निकायतो।
अङ्गतो च नवविधं, धम्मक्खन्धगणनतो।
चतुरासीतिसहस्स-धम्मक्खन्धपभेदनं[1] ति॥

पिटक-वसेन बुद्ध-वचनं

कथं पिटकतो? पिटकं हि तिविधं होति। विनय-पिटकं, अभिधम्म पिटकं, सुत्तन्त-पिटकं ति।

तत्थ कतमं विनयपिटकं? पाराजिक-कण्डं, पाचित्तिय-कण्डं, महावग्ग-कण्डं, चुल्लवग्ग-कण्डं, परिवार-कण्डं ति। इमानि कण्डानि विनयपिटकं नाम।

---

१. भेदं म.१

कतमं अभिधम्मपिटकं ? धम्मसङ्गणि-पकरणं, विभङ्ग-पकरणं, धातुकथा-पकरणं, पञ्ञत्ति-पकरणं, कथावत्थु-पकरणं, यमक-पकरणं, पट्ठान-पकरणं। इमानि सत्त पकरणानि अभिधम्म-पिटकं नाम।

कतमं सुत्तन्त-पिटकं नाम ? सीलक्खन्धवग्गादिकं, अवसेसं बुद्ध-वचनं सुत्तन्त-पिटकं नाम।

निकाय-वसेन बुद्ध-वचनं

R.56 कथं निकायतो पञ्चविधा होति ? दीघनिकायो, मज्झिम-निकायो, संयुत्तनिकायो, अङ्गुत्तरनिकायो, खुद्दकनिकायो ति।

तत्थ कतमो दीघनिकायो ? सीलक्खन्धवग्गो, महावग्गो, पाधियवग्गो[1] ति इमे तयो वग्गा दीघनिकायो नाम। इमेसु तीसु वग्गेसु चतुतिंस सुत्तानि च होन्ति।

५. चतुतिंसेव सुत्तन्ता, सीलक्खन्धवग्गादिका।
यस्स भवन्ति सो येव, दीघनिकायो नाम होति ॥

कतमो मज्झिमनिकायो ? मूलपण्णासो, मज्झिमपण्णासो, उपरिपण्णासो ति इमे तयो पण्णासा मज्झिमनिकायो नाम। इमेसु तीसु पण्णासेसु पण्णासधिकसुत्तसतानि होन्ति।

६. दियड्ढसतसुत्तन्ता, द्विसुत्तं यस्स सन्ति सो।
मज्झिम निकायो नाम, मूलपण्णास-आदिको[2] ति ॥

कतमो संयुत्तनिकायो ? सगाथावग्गो, निदानवग्गो, सलाय-तनवग्गो खन्धकवग्गो, महावग्गो ति इमे पञ्च वग्गा संयुत्तनिकायो

१. पावि० म. २
२. पन्ना समा० म. २

नाम। इमेसु पञ्चेसु वग्गेसु द्वासट्ठिसत्तसताधिकसत्तसुत्तसहस्सानि होन्ति।

७. द्वासट्ठिसत्तसतानि, सत्त सहस्सकानि च।
सुत्तानि यस्स होन्ति, सो सगाथादिक वग्गिको।
संयुत्तनिकायो नाम, विदितब्बो विञ्ञूना ति॥

कतमो अङ्गुत्तरनिकायो ? एक्कनिपातो, दुक्कनिपातो, तिक्कनिपातो, चतुक्कनिपातो, पञ्चनिपातो, छक्कनिपातो, सत्तनिपातो, अट्ठनिपातो, नवनिपातो, दसनिपातो, एकादसनिपातो ति इमे एकादस निपाता अङ्गुत्तरनिकायो नाम। इमेसु एकादससु निपातेसुसत्तपण्णास-पञ्चसताधिकनवसुत्तसहस्सानि होन्ति।

८. नवसुत्तसहस्सानि, पञ्चसुत्तसतानि च।
सत्तपण्णासाधिकानि, सुत्तानि यस्स होन्ति।
सो अङ्गुत्तरनिकायो ति, एकनिपातादिको ति॥

R.57 कतमो खुद्दकनिकायो ? खुद्दकपाठो, धम्मपदं, उदानं, इतिवुत्तकं, सुत्तनिपातो, विमानवत्थु, पेतवत्थु, थेरगाथा, थेरीगाथा, जातकं, निद्देसो, पटिसम्भिदामग्गो, अपदान, बुद्धवंसो, चरिया पिटकं, विनयपिटकं, अभिधम्मपिटकं ति अयं खुद्दकनिकायो। इमेसु गन्धेसु अनेकानि सुत्तसहस्सानि होन्ति।

९. अनेकानि सुत्तसहस्सानि, निद्दिट्ठानि महेसिना।
निकाये पञ्चमे रम्मे, खुद्दको ति विसुतो ति॥

अंग-वसेन बुद्ध-वचनं

कथं अङ्गतो ? अङ्गं हि नवविधं होति। सुत्तं, गेय्यं, वेय्याकरणं, गाथा, उदानं, इतिवुत्तकं, जातकं, अब्भुतधम्मं, वेदल्लं ति नवप्पभेदं होति। तत्थ उभतोविभङ्गनिद्देसे, खन्धकपरिवारा,

सुत्तनिपाते मङ्गलसुत्तं, रतनसुत्तं, नालकसुत्त तुवट्टकसुत्तानि अञ्ञं पि सुत्तनामकं तथागतवचनं सुत्तं ति वेदितब्बं। सब्बं पि सगाथकं गेय्यं ति वेदितब्बं ति। विसेसेन संयुत्तके सकलो पि सगाथावग्गो गेय्यं ति वेदितब्बं। सकलं अभिधम्मपिटकं, निगाथकं सुत्तं च, यं च अञ्ञं पि अट्ठहि अङ्गेहि असंगहितं बुद्धवचनं तं बुद्धवचनं वेय्याकरणं वेदितब्बं। धम्मपद, थेरगाथा, थेरीगाथा, सुत्तनिपाते नोसुत्तनामिका सुद्धिकगाथा च गाथा ति वेदितब्बा। सोमनस्स-ञाणमयिक गाथापटिसंयुत्ता द्वे असीतिसुत्तन्ता उदानं ति वेदितब्बं ति। 'वुत्तं हि एतं भगवता' ति आदिनयपवत्तो द्वादसुत्तरसतसुत्तन्ता इतिवुत्तकं ति वेदितब्बा। अपण्णकजातकादीनि पण्णासाधिकानि पञ्चजातकसतानि जातकं ति वेदितब्बा। चत्तारो मे, भिक्खवे, अच्छरिया अब्भुत धम्मा सन्ति[1] इति आदि नयप्पवत्ता सब्बे पि अच्छरिय-अब्भुतधम्मपटिसंयुत्ता सुत्तन्ता अब्भुतधम्मं ति वेदितब्बं। चुल्लवेदल्ल-महावेदल्ल-सम्मादिट्ठि-सक्कपञ्ह-संखारभाजनीय-महा-पुण्णमसुत्तन्तादयो सब्बे पि वेदं च तुट्ठिं च लद्धा लद्धा पुच्छित-सुत्तन्ता वेदल्लं ति वेदितब्बं।

धम्मक्खन्ध-वसेन बुद्ध-वचनं

R.58 कतमानि चतुरासीति धम्मक्खन्धसहस्सानि ? दुजानाति। चतुरासीति धम्मक्खन्धसहस्सानि सचे वित्थारेन कथिस्सं अति-पपञ्चो भविस्सति, तस्मा नयवसेन कथिस्सामि। एकं वत्थुं धम्म-क्खन्धो, एकं निदानं एको धम्मक्खन्धो, एकं पण्हापुच्छनं एको धम्मक्खन्धो, एकं पञ्हाविसज्जनं एको धम्मक्खन्धो।

चतुरासीति धम्मक्खन्धसहस्सानि केन भासितानि, कत्थ भासितानीति, कदा भासितानि, कं आरब्भ भासितानि, किं अत्थं

---

१. आनन्दे ति—म. २

भासितानि, केन धारितानि, केन आभतानि, किं अत्थं परियपुणितब्बानीति, अयं पुच्छा उद्धरितब्बा ।

तत्रायं विसज्जना । केन भासितानीति बुद्धेन च बुद्धानुबुद्धेहि च भासितानि । कत्थ भासितानीति देवेसु च मनुस्सेसु च भासितानि । कदा भासितानीति भगवतो धरमानकाले च भासितानि । कं आरब्भ भासितानीति पञ्चवग्गियादिके वेनेय्यवन्धवे आरब्भ भासितानि । किं अत्थं भासितानीति वज्जं च अवज्जं च ञत्वा वज्जं पहाय अवज्जे पटिपज्जित्वा निब्बानपरियन्ते दिट्ठधम्मिकसम्परायिकत्ते सम्पापुणितुं । केन धारितानीति, अनुबुद्धेहि चेव सिस्सानुसिस्सेहि च धारितानि । केन आभतानीति आचरियपरम्परेहि आभतानि । किं अत्थं परियापुणितब्बानीति वज्जं च अवज्जं च ञत्वा वज्जं पहाय अवज्जे पटिपज्जित्वा निब्बानपरियन्ते दिट्ठधम्मिकसम्परायिकत्ते सम्पापुणितुं करुणाय आभतानि । ते सदेवताय निब्बानपरियन्ते दिट्ठधम्मिकसम्परायिकत्थे साधिकानि होन्ति । ते तत्थ केहि अप्पमत्तेन परियापुणितब्बानि धारेतब्बानि वाचेतब्बानि सज्झायं कातब्बानीति ।

इति चुल्लगन्धवंसे पिटकत्तयदीपको नाम

पठमो परिच्छेदो ।

दुतियो परिच्छेदो

गन्धकारक-आचरिय-वण्णना

आचरिया पन अत्थि पोराणाचरिया, अत्थि अट्ठकथाचरिया, अत्थि गन्धकारकाचरिया, अत्थि तिविधनामकाचरिया ।

कतमे पोराणाचरिया ? पठम-संगायनायं पञ्चसता खीणासवा, पञ्चन्नं निकायानं नामं च, अत्थं च, अधिप्पायं च, पदं च, ब्यञ्जनं च, सोधनकिच्चं[1] अनवसेसं करिंसु[2] । दुतिय-संगाय-
R.59 नायं सत्त सता खीणासवा तेसं येव सद्दत्थादिकं किच्चं पुन करिंसु । ततिय-संगायनायं सहस्समत्ता खीणासवा तेसं येव सद्दत्थादिकं किच्चं पुन करिंसु । इच्चेवं द्वे सताधिका द्वेसहस्सखीणासवा महाकच्चायनं ठपेत्वा अवसेसा पोराणाचरिया नाम ।

ये पोराणाचरिया ते येव अट्ठकथाचरिया नाम ।

कतमे गन्धकारकाचरिया ? महाबुद्धघोसादयो अनेकाचरिया गन्धकारकाचरिया नाम ।

कतमे तिविधनामकाचरिया ? महाकच्चायनो तिविधनामो ।[3]

कतमे गन्धे कच्चायनेन कता ? कच्चायनगन्धो, महानिरूतिगन्धो, चुल्लनिरूत्तिगन्धो, नेत्तिगन्धो, पेटकोपदेसगन्धो वण्णनीतिगन्धो[4]ति इमे छ गन्धा महाकच्चायनेन कता ।

---

१. सोधनं—म. २

२. किच्चं—म. २

३. तिविधा—म. १

४. म. १ पोत्थके नत्थि ।

कतमे अनेकाचरियेहि कता ? गन्धाचरियो कुरून्दीगन्धं नाम अकासि। अञ्ञतरो आचरियो महापच्चरियं नाम अट्ठकथं अकासि। अञ्ञतरो आचरियो कुरून्दीगन्धस्स अट्ठकथं अकासि।

महाबुद्धघोसो नामाचरियो विसुद्धिमग्गो, दीघनिकायस्स सुमंगलविलासीनी नाम अट्ठकथा, मज्झिमनिकायस्स पपञ्चसूदनी नाम अट्ठकथा, संयुत्तनिकायस्स सारत्थपकासनी नाम अट्ठकथा, अङ्गुत्तरनिकायस्स मनोरथपुरणी नाम अट्ठकथा, पञ्चविनयगन्धानं समन्तपासादिका नाम अट्ठकथा, सत्तअभिधम्मगन्धानं परमत्थकथा नाम अट्ठकथा, पातिमोक्खसंखायमातिकाय कङ्खावितरणी नाम अट्ठकथा, धम्मपदस्स अट्ठकथा, जातकस्स अट्ठकथा, खुद्दकपाठस्स अट्ठकथा, सुत्तनिपातस्स अट्ठकथा[1] अपदानस्स अट्ठकथा ति इमे तेरस गन्धे अकासि।

R.60 बुद्धदत्तो नामाचरियो विनियविनिच्छयो, उत्तरविनिच्छयो, अभिधम्मावतारो, बुद्धवंसस्स मधुरत्थविलासिनी नाम अट्ठकथा ति इमे चत्तारो गन्धे अकासि।

आनन्दो नामाचरियो सत्ताभिधम्मगन्धअट्ठकथाय मूलटीकं नाम टीकं अकासि।

धम्मपालाचरियो नेत्तिपकरणअट्ठकथा, इतिवुत्तकअट्टकथा, उदानअट्ठकथा, चरियापिटकअट्ठकथा, थेरगाथाठ्ठकथा, थेरीगाथाट्ठकथा,[2] विमानवत्थुस्स विमलविलासिनी नाम अट्ठकथा, पेतवत्थुस्स विमलविलासिनी नाम अट्ठकथा, विसुद्धिमग्गस्स परमत्थमञ्जूसा नाम टीका, दीघनिकायाट्ठकथादीनं चतुन्नं अट्ठकथानं लीनत्थपकासिनी नाम टीका, जातक-अट्ठकथाय लीनत्थपकासिनी नाम टीका,

---

१. रोमन पोत्थके नत्थि।

२. रोमन पोत्थके नत्थि।

नेत्ति-अट्ठकथाय टीका, बुद्धवंसट्ठकथाय परमत्थदीपनी नाम टीका, नाम अभिधम्मट्ठकथायटीकाय लीनत्थवण्णना अनुटीका ति इमे चुद्दसमत्ते गन्धे अकासि ।

द्वे पुब्बाचरिया निरूत्तिमञ्जूसा नाम चुल्लनिरूत्तिटीकं च महानिरूत्तिसंखेपं च अकंसु ।

महावजिरबुद्धि[1] नामाचरियो विनयगण्धि नाम पकरणं अकासि ।

विमलबुद्धि-नामाचरियो मुखमत्तदीपनी नाम न्यासपकरणं अकासि ।

चुल्लवजिरो नामाचरियो अत्थब्यक्ख्यानं नाम पकरणं अकासि ।

दीपकंरो नामाचरियो रूपसिद्धिपकरणं, रूपसिद्धिटीकं, सुम्मपञ्चसुत्तं चेति तिविधपकरणं अकासि ।

आनन्दाचरियस्स जेट्ठसिस्सो चुल्लधम्मपालो नामाचरियो सच्चसंखेपं नाम अकासि ।

R. 61 कस्सपो नामाचरियो मोहविच्छेदनी, विमतिच्छेदनी, बुद्धवंसो, अनागतवंसो ति चतुब्बिधं पकरणं अकासि ।

महानामो नामाचरियो सद्धम्मपकासनी नाम पटिसम्भिदामग्गस्स अट्ठकथं अकासि ।

दीपवंसो, बोधिवंसो, चुल्लवंसो, महावंसो, पटिसम्भिदामग्गट्ठकथाय गण्ढि चेति इमे पञ्च[2] गन्धा आचरियेहि[3] विसुं विसुं कता ।

---

१. वचिरबुद्धिकायो—म० २

२ छ—म० २

३. महा० म. २

नवो महानामो नामाचरियो महावंसं, चुल्लवंसं नाम द्वे पकरणं अकासि।

उपसेनो नामाचरियो सद्धम्मट्ठितिकं नाम महानिद्देसस्स अट्ठकथं अकासि।

मोग्गलानो नामाचरियो मोग्गलानब्याकरणं नाम ब्याकरणं अकासि।

संघरक्खितो नामाचरियो सुबोधालंकारं नाम पकरणं अकासि।

वुत्तोदयकारो नामाचरियो वुत्तोदयं नाम पकरण, सम्बन्ध-चिन्ता नाम पकरणं, खुद्दसिक्खाय नवटीकं अकासि।

धम्मसिरी नामाचरियो खुद्दसिक्खं नाम पकरणं अकासि।

खुद्दसिक्खाय पुराणटीका, मूलसिक्खाटीका चेति इमे द्वे गन्धा द्वेहि आचरियेहि विसुं विसुं कता।

अनुरूद्धो नामाचरियो परमत्थविनिच्छयं, नामरूपपरि-च्छेदं, अभिधम्मत्थसंगहपकरणं चेति तिविधं पकरणं अकासि।

खेमो नामाचरियो खेमं नाम पकरणं अकासि।

सारिपुत्तो नामाचरियो विनयट्ठकथाय सारत्थदीपनी नाम टीकं, विनय-संगहपकरणं, विनयसंगहस्स टीकं, अङ्गुत्तरट्ठकथाय सारत्थमञ्जूसं नाम टीकं, पञ्चकं चेति इमे पञ्च गन्धे अकासि।

R .62 बुद्धनागो नामाचरियो विनयत्थमञ्जूसं नाम कङ्खावितर-णिया टीकं अकासि।

नवो मोग्गल्लानो नामाचरियो अभिधानप्पदीपिकं नाम पकरणं अकासि।

वचिस्सरो नामाचरियो महासामी नाम सुबोधालंकारस्स टीका, वुत्तोदयविवरणं, सुमङ्गलपसादनी नाम खुद्दसिक्खाय टीका, सम्बन्धचिन्ताय टीका, बालावतारो, मोग्गलानब्याकरणस्स टीका, पञ्चिकाय टीका, योगविनिच्छयो, विनयविनिच्छयस्स टीका, उत्तर-विनिच्छयस्स टीका, नामरूपपरिच्छेदस्स टीका, सद्दत्थस्स पदरूप विभावनं, खेमपकरणस्स टीका, सीमालङ्कारो, मूलसिक्खाय टीका, रूपारूपविभागो, पच्चयसङ्गहो, सच्चसङ्खेपस्स टीका चेति इमा अट्ठारस गन्धे अकासि ।

सुमङ्गलो नामाचरियो अभिधम्मावतारगन्धस्स टीकं अभि-धम्मत्थविकासनी, अभिधम्मसंगहस्स टीकं च अभिधम्मत्थविभावनी दुविधं पकरणं अकासि ।

धम्मकित्ति नामाचरियो दन्तधातुपकरणं (अकासि) ।

मेधंकरो नामाचरियो जिनचरितं नाम पकरणं अकासि ।

कङ्खवितरणिया लिनत्थपकासिनी, निसन्देहो, धम्मनु-सारनी, ञेय्यासन्दति, ञेय्यासन्दतिया टीका, सुमहावतारो, लोक-पञ्ञत्तिपकरणं, तथागतुप्पत्तिपकरणं, नलातधातुवण्णना, सीहल-वत्थु, धम्मपदीपको, पटिपत्तिसङ्गहो, विसुद्धिमग्गगण्धि, अभिधम्म-गण्धि, नेत्तिपकरणगण्धि, विसुद्धिमग्गचुल्लटीका, सोतप्पमालिनी,
R. 63 पसादनी, ओकासलोकसूदनी, सुबोधलंकारस्स नवटीका चेति इमे
वीसति गन्धा वीसताचरियेहि विसुं विसुं कता ।

सद्धम्मसिरी नामाचरियो सद्दत्थभेदचिन्ता नाम पकरणं अकासि ।

देवो नामाचरियो सुमणकूटवण्णना नाम पकरणं अकासि ।

चुल्लबुद्धघोसो नामाचरियो जातत्तगीनिदानं, सोतत्तगी-निदानं नाम द्वे पकरणं अकासि ।

रट्ठपालो नामाचरियो मधुरसवाहिनी[1] नाम पकरणं अकासि।

सुभूतचन्दनो नामाचरियो लिङ्गत्थविवरणपकरणं अकासि।

अग्गवंसो नामाचरियो सद्दनीतिपकरणं नाम अकासि।

विमलबुद्धि नामाचरियो न्यासपकरणस्स महाटीकं नाम अकासि।

गुणसागरो[2] नामाचरियो मुखमत्तसारं, तट्टीकं च दुविधं पकरणं अकासि।

अभयो नामाचरियो सद्दत्थभेदचिन्ताय महाटीकं अकासि।

ञाणसागरो नामाचरियो लिङ्गत्थविवरणपकरणं अकासि।

अञ्ञतरो आचरियो गूळ्हत्थटीकं, बालप्पबोधनं च दुविधं पकरणं अकासि।

अञ्ञतरो आचरियो सद्दत्थभेदचिन्ताय मज्झिमटीकं अकासि।

उत्तमो नामाचरियो बालावतारटीकं लिङ्गत्थविवरणटीकं च दुविधं पकरणं इति अकासि।

अञ्ञतरो आचरियो सद्दभेदचिन्ताय नवटीकं अकासि।

एको अमच्चो अभिधानप्पदीपिकाय टीकं, दण्डीपकरणस्स मगधभूतं टीकं, कोलधजनस्स सकटभासाय टीकं च तिविधं पकरणं अकासि।

धम्मसेनापति नामाचरियो कारिकं, एतिमासमिदीपिकं, मनोहारां च तिविधं पकरणं अकासि।

---

१. संगाहीतिकित्ति—म० २

२. सागरो—म० २

R. 64 अञ्ञतरो आचरियो कारिकाय टीकं अकासि।

अञ्ञतरो आचरियो एतिमासमिदीपिकाय टीकं अकासि।

क्यच्वारञ्ञो सद्दबिन्दु नाम पकरणं परमत्थबिन्दुपकरणं अकासि।

सद्धम्मगुरु नामाचरियो सद्दवुत्तिपकासनं नाम पकरणं अकासि।

सारिपुत्तो नामाचरियो सद्दवुत्तिपकासकस्स टीकं अकासि।

अञ्ञतरो आचरियो कच्चायनभेदं च कच्चायनसारं कच्चायनसारस्स टीकं च तिविधं पकरणं अकासि।

नवो मेधंकरो नामाचरियो लोकदीपकसारं नाम पकरणं अकासि।

अग्गपण्डितो नामाचरियो लोकुप्पत्ति नाम पकरणं अकासि।

चीवरो नामाचरियो जङ्घदासस्स टीकं अकासि।

मातिकत्थदीपनी, सीमालंकारस्स टीका, विनयसमुट्ठानदीपनी, गन्धसारो, पट्ठानगणनानयो, अभिधम्मत्थसङ्गहस्स सङ्खेपवण्णना नवटीका, कच्चायनस्स सुत्तनिद्देसो, पाटिमोक्खविसोधनी चेति अट्ठ गन्धे सद्धम्मजोतिपालाचरियो अकासि।

नवो विमलबुद्धि नामाचरियो अभिधम्मपण्णरसट्ठानं पकरणं अकासि।

वेपुल्लबद्धि नामाचरियो सद्दसारत्थजालिनिया टीका, वुत्तोदयटीका, परमत्थमञ्जूसा नाम अभिधम्मसंगहटीकाय अनुटीका, दसगण्धिवण्णना नाम मगधभूताविदग्गं, विदधिमुक्खमण्डनटीका चेति इमे छ गन्धे अकासि।

अञ्ञतरो आचरियो पञ्चपकरणटीकाय नवानुटीकं अकासि।

R. 65 अरियवंसो नामाचरियो अभिधम्मसंगहटीकाय मणिसारमञ्जूसं नाम नवानुटीकं, द्वारकथाय टीकाय मणिदीपं नाम

नवानुटीकं, गण्डाभरणं, च महानिस्सरं, च जातकविसोधनं च इति इमे पञ्च गन्धे अकासि।

पेटकोपदेसस्स टीकं उदुम्बरनामाचरियो अकासि।

तं पन पकुधनगरवासी अभिधम्मसंगहस्स टीका, चतुभाणवारस्स अट्ठकथा, महासारपकासनी, महादीपनी, सारत्थदीपनी, गतिपकरणं, हत्थसारो, भुम्मसंगहो, भूम्मनिद्देसो, दसवत्थु, कायविरतिटीका, जोतना, निरुत्ति, विभत्तिकथा, सद्धम्मपालिनी, पञ्चगतिवण्णना, बालचित्तपबोधनी, धम्मचक्कसुत्तस्स नवट्ठकथा, दण्डधातुपकरणस्स टीका चेति इमे बीसति गन्धा नानाचरियेहि कता। अञ्ञानि पकरणानि अत्थि। कतमानि? सद्धम्मपालनं, बालप्पबोधनपकरणस्स टीका, च जिनालंकारपकरणस्स नवटीका, च लिङ्गत्थविनिच्छयो, पातिमोक्खविवरणं, परमत्थविवरणं, कथाविवरणं, समन्तपासादिकविवरणं, अभिधम्मत्थसंगहविवरणं, सच्चसंखेपविवरणं, सद्दत्थभेदचिन्ताविवरणं, कच्चायनसारविवरणं, अभिधम्मत्थसंगहस्स टीकाविवरणं, महावेस्सन्तरजातकस्स विवरणं, सक्काभिमतं, महावेस्सन्तरजातकस्स नवट्ठकथा, पठमसम्बोधि, लोकनीति च बुद्धघोसाचरियनिदानं, मिलिन्दपण्हावण्णना, चतुरारक्खाय अट्ठकथा, सद्दावुत्तिपकरणस्स नवटीकं, इच्चेवं पञ्चवीसति पमाणानि लंकादीपादीसु ठानेसु पण्डितेहि कतानि अहेसुं।

R. 66 सम्बुद्धे गाथा, च, नरदेव नाम गाथा च यदा हवे चीवरत्थि गाथा च, वीसति ओवादगाथा च, दानसत्थरि, सीलसत्थरि, सब्बदानवण्णना, अनन्तबुद्धवण्णनागाथा च, अट्ठवीसति बुद्धवन्दनागाथा च अतीतानागतपच्चुप्पन्नबुद्धवण्णनागाथा च असीतिमहासावकवण्णनागाथा च नवहारगुणवण्णना चा इति इमे बुद्धपणामगाथायो पण्डितेहि लंकादीपादीसु ठानेसु कता अहेसुं।

इति चुल्लगन्धवंसे गन्धकारकाचरियदीपको
नाम दुतियो परिच्छेदो।

ततियो परिच्छेदो

आचरियानं संजातट्ठान दीपको

आचरियेसु च अत्थि जम्बूदीपिकाचरिया, अत्थि लंकादीपिकाचरिया। कतमे जम्बुदीपिकाचरिया, कतमे लंकादीपिकाचरिया ?

महाकच्चायनो जम्बुदीपिकाचरियो। सो हि अवन्तिरट्ठे उज्जेनीनगरे चन्दपच्चोतस-नाम रञ्ञो पुरोहितो हुत्वा कामानं आदीनवं दिस्वा घरावासं पहाय सत्थु सासने पब्बज्जित्वा हेट्ठावुत्तपकारे गन्धे अकासि।

महाअट्ठकथाचरियो, महापच्चरिकाचरियो, च महाकुरुन्दिकाचरियो, अञ्ञतराचरियेहि इमे पञ्चारियो लंकादीपिकाचरियो नाम। ते हि बुद्धघोसाचरियस्स पुरे भूता, चिरे काले अहेसुं।

महाबुद्धघोसाचरियो जम्बुदीपिको। सो किर मगधरट्ठे संगामरञ्ञो पुरोहितस्स केसी नाम ब्रह्मणस्स पुत्तो सत्थु सासने पब्बज्जित्वा लंकादीपं गतो, हेट्ठावुत्तप्पकारे गन्धे अकासि।

बुद्धदत्ताचरियो, आनन्दाचरियो, धम्मपालाचरियो, द्वे पुब्बाचरिया, महावजिरबुद्धाचरियो, चुल्लवजिरबुद्धाचरियो, दीपकंराचरियो, चुल्लधम्मपालाचरियो, कस्सपाचरियो'ति इमे दस आचरिया जम्बुदीपिका हेट्ठावुत्तप्पकारे गन्धे अकंसु।

R.67 महानामाचरियो, अञ्ञतराचरियो, चुल्लनामाचरियो, उपसेनाचरियो, मोग्गलानाचरियो, संघरक्खिताचरियो, वाचिस्सराचरियो, वुत्तोदयकाचरियो, धम्मपालाचरियो, अञ्ञतरा द्वाचरिया, अनुरुद्धाचरियो, खेमाचरियो, सारिपुत्ताचरियो, बद्धनागाचरियो, चुल्लमोग्गलानाचरियो, वाचितस्स पाचरियो, सुमङ्गलाचरियो, बुद्धपियाचरियो, एकाचरियो, मेधंकराचरियो, अग्गपण्डिताचरियो, वजिराचरियो, सद्धम्मपालाचरियो, नवो विमलबुद्धाचरियो, इति इमे तेवीसति आचरिया जम्बुदीपिका हेट्ठावुत्तप्पकारे गन्धे पुक्कामसंखाते अरिमद्दनानगरे अंकसु ।

नवो विमलबुद्धाचरियो जम्बुदीपिको हेट्ठावुत्तप्पकारे गन्धे पन्यनगरे अंकसु । अञ्ञतराचरियो अरियवंसाचरियो'ति इमे द्वाचरिया जम्बुदीपिका हेट्ठाबुत्तप्पकारे गन्धे अवन्तिपुरे अंकसु ।

अञ्ञतरा वीसताचरिया जम्बुदीपिका हेट्ठावुत्तप्पकारे गन्धे काञ्चिपुरनगरे अंकसु ।

इति चुल्लगन्धवंसे आचरियानं संजातट्ठानदीपिको
नाम ततियो परिच्छेदो ।

चतुत्थो परिच्छेदो

गन्धकारकाचरियदीपको

गन्धो पन सिया आयाचनेन आचरियेहि कता सिया अनावाचनेन आचरियेहि कता ।

कतमे गन्धा[1] आयाचनेन, कतमे[2] अनायाचनेन कता ?

महाकच्चायनाचरियगन्धा

महाकच्चायनगन्धो, महाअट्ठकथागन्धो, महापच्चरियगन्धो, महाकुरुन्दीगन्धो, महापच्चरियगन्धस्स अट्ठकथागन्धो, इमे छ गन्धे हि आचरियेहि अत्तनो मतिया सासनवुड्ढि-अत्थाय सद्धम्मट्ठितिया कता ।

महाकच्चायनाचरियगन्धदीपना निट्ठिता ।

बुद्धघोसाचरियगन्धा

बुद्धघोसाचरियगन्धेसु पन विसुद्धिमग्गो संघपालेन नाम आयाचितेन बुद्धघोसाचरियेनो कतो ।

दीघनिकायस्स अट्ठकथागन्धो दाट्ठनामेन संघत्थेरेन आयाचितेन बुद्धघोसाचरियेन कतो ।

मज्झिमनिकायस्स अट्ठकथागन्धो बुद्धमित्तनामेन थेरेन आयाचितेन बुद्धघोसाचरियेन कतो ।

---

१. गन्धे—म० १

२. गन्धे—म० १

संयुत्तनिकायस्स अट्ठकथागन्धो जोतिपालेन नाम थेरेन आयाचितेन बुद्धघोसाचरियेन कतो।

अङ्गुत्तरनिकायस्स अट्ठकथागन्धो भद्दन्तनामत्थेरेन सह आजीवकेन आयाचितेन बुद्धघोसाचरियेन कतो।

समन्तपासादिका नाम अट्ठकथागन्धो बुद्धसिरी नामेन थेरेन आयाचितेन बुद्धघोसाचरियेन कतो।

सत्तनं अभिधम्मगन्धानं अट्ठकथागन्धो चुल्लबुद्धघोसो नाम भिक्खुना आयाचितेन बुद्धघोसाचरियेन कतो।

धम्मपदस्स अट्ठकथागन्धो कुमारकस्सपनामेन थेरेन आयाचितेन बुद्धघोसाचरियेन कतो।

जातकस्स अट्ठकथागन्धो अत्थदस्सीबुद्धमित्तबुद्धपियसंखातेहि तीहि थेरेहि आयाचितेन बुद्धघोसाचरियेन कतो।

खुद्दकपाठस्स अट्ठकथागन्धो सुत्तनिपातस्स अट्ठकथागन्धो अत्तनो मतिया बुद्धघोसाचरियेन कता।

R. 69 अपदानस्स अट्ठकथागन्धो पञ्चनिकायविञ्ञूहि पञ्चहि थेरेहि आयाचितेन बुद्धघोसाचरियेन कतो।

पातिमोक्खस्स अट्ठकथा कङ्खावितरणीगन्धो अत्तनो मतिया बुद्धघोसाचरियेन कतो।

बुद्धघोसाचरियगन्धदीपना निट्ठिता।

बुद्धदत्ताचरियगन्धा

बुद्धदत्ताचरियगन्धेसु पन विनयविनिच्छयगन्धो अत्तनो सिस्सेन बुद्धसीहेन[1] नाम थेरेन आयाचितेन बुद्धदत्ताचरियेन कतो।

उत्तरविनिच्छयगन्धो सङ्घपालेन नाम थेरेन आयाचितेन धम्मकित्ति-आचरियो, मेधंकराचरियो, बुद्धरक्खिताचरियो, उप-

---

१. सुमति—म० १

तिस्साचरियो, अञ्ञतरा विसताचरिया, सद्धम्मचाराचरियो, देवाचरियो, चुल्लबुद्धघोसाचरियो, सारिपुत्ताचरियो, रट्ठपालाचरियो'ति इमे एकपण्णासाचरिया लंकादीपिकाचरिया नाम।

सुभूतचन्दनाचरियो, अग्गवंसाचरियो, नवो वजिरबुद्धाचरियो, वेपुल्लबुद्धाचरियो, गुणसागराचरियो, अभयाचरियो, ञाणसागराचरियो, धम्मपालाचरियो, अञ्ञतरा द्वाचरिया, उत्तमाचरियो, अञ्ञतरो आचरियो, चतुरङ्गबलमहामच्चो, धम्मसेनापताचरियो, अञ्ञतरा तयो आचरिया, क्यच्वारञ्ञो च सद्धम्मगुरुआचरियो, सारिपुत्ताचरियो, धम्माभिनन्दाचरियो, अञ्ञतरो बुद्धदत्ताचरियेन कतो।

अभिधम्मावतारो नाम गन्धो अत्तनो सिस्सेन सुमति नामत्थेरेन आयाचितेन बुद्धदत्ताचरियेन कतो।

बुद्धवंसस्स अट्ठकथागन्धो तेन एव बुद्धसीह नामत्थेरेन आयाचितेन बुद्धदत्ताचरियेन कतो।

जिनालंकारगन्धो संघपालत्थेरेन आयाचितेन बुद्धदत्ताचरियेन कतो।

बुद्धदत्ताचरियगन्धादीपना निट्ठिता।

आनन्दाचरियगन्धा

अभिधम्मत्थकथाय मूलटीका नाम टीकागन्धो बुद्धमित्तनामत्थेरेन आयाचितेन आनन्दाचरियेन कतो।

आनन्दाचरियगन्धदीपना निट्ठिता।

धम्मपालाचरियगन्धा

नेत्तिपकरणस्स अट्ठकथागन्धो धम्मरक्खितनामत्थेरेन आयाचितेन धम्मपालाचरियेन कतो।

इतिवुत्तकट्ठकथागन्धो, उदानट्ठकथागन्धो, चरियापिटकट्ठकथागन्धो, थेरगाथाट्ठकथागन्धो, थेरीगाथाट्ठकथागन्धो, विमानवत्थुपेतवत्थुट्ठकथागन्धो इमे सत्त गन्धा अत्तनो मतिया धम्मपालाचरियेन कता।

विसुद्धिमग्गटीकागन्धो दाठानामेन थेरेन आयाचितेन धम्मपालाचरियेन कतो।

दीघनिकायट्ठकथादीनं चतुन्नं अट्ठकथानं टीकागन्धो अभिधम्मट्ठकथाय अनुटीकागन्धो, जातकट्ठकथाय टीकागन्धो, निरुत्तिपकरणट्ठकथाय टीकागन्धो, बुद्धवंसट्ठकथाय टीकागन्धो इति इमे पञ्च गन्धा अत्तनो मतिया धम्मपालाचरियेन कता।

धम्मपालाचरियगन्धदीपना निट्ठिता।

अञ्ञाचरिय-गन्धा

R. 70 निरुत्तिमञ्जूसा नाम चूलटीकागन्धो महानिरुत्तिसंखेपो नाम गन्धो च अत्तनो मतिया पुब्बाचरियेहि विसुं विसुं कता।

पञ्चविनयपकरणस्स विनयगण्धि नाम गन्धो अत्तनो मतिया महावजिरबुद्धिआचरियेन कता।

न्याससंखातो मुखमत्तदीपनी नाम गन्धो अत्तनो मतिया विमलबुद्धिआचरियेन कतो।

अत्थब्याक्खयानो नाम गन्धो अत्तनो मतिया चुल्लविमलबुद्धाचरियेन कतो।

रुपसिद्धिगन्धस्स टीकागन्धो सम्पपञ्चसत्ती[1] च अत्तनो मतिया दीपंकराचरियेन कतो।

१. सम्मपञ्च – म० १

सच्चसंखेपो नाम गन्धो अत्तनो मतिया चुल्लधम्मपालचरियेन कतो।

मोहविच्छेदनीगन्धो विमतिच्छेदनीगन्धो अत्तनो मतिया कस्सपाचरियेन कतो।

पटिसम्भिदामग्गट्ठकथागन्धो महानामेन उपासकेन आयाचितेन महानामाचरियेन कतो।

दीपवंसो थूपवंसो बोधिवंसो चूल्लवंसो पोराणवंसो महावंसो चा'ति इमे छ गन्धा अत्तनो मतिया महाचरियेहि विसुं विसुं कता।

नवो[1] वंसो[1] गन्धो[1] अत्तनो मतिया[1] चुल्लमहानामाचरियेन[1] कतो।

सद्धम्मपज्जोतिका नाम महानिद्देसस्सट्ठकथागन्धो देवेन नाम थेरेन आयाचितेन उपसेनाचरियेन कतो।

मोग्गलानब्याकरणगन्धो अत्तनो मतिया मोग्गलानाचरियेन कतो।

सुबोधालंकरो नाम गन्धो वुत्तोदयो[2] नाम[2] गन्धो[2] अत्तनो मतिया संघरक्खिताचरियेन कतो।

वुत्तोदयगन्धो अत्तनो मतिया वुत्तोदयकाराचरियेन कतो।[3]

खुद्दसिक्खा नाम गन्धो अत्तनो मतिया धम्मसिराचरियेन कतो।

---

१. म० १ पोत्थके नत्थि।

२ म० १ पोत्थके नत्थि।

३. म० १ पोत्थके नत्थि।

R. 71 पोराणखुद्दसिक्खाटीका च मूलसिक्खाटीका चा' ति इमे द्वे गन्धा अत्तनो मतिया अञ्ञतरेहि द्विहि आचरियेहि विसुं कता।

परमत्थविनिच्छयो नाम गन्धो संघरक्खितत्थेरेन आयाचितेन अनुरुद्धाचरियेन कतो।

नामरूपपरिच्छेदो नाम गन्धो अत्तनो मतिया अनुरुद्धाचरियेन कतो।

अभिधम्मत्थसंगहो नाम गन्धो नम्भनामेन[1] उपासकेन आयाचितेनो अनुरुद्धाचरियेन कतो।

खेमो नाम गन्धो अत्तनो मतिया खेमाचरियेन कतो।

सारत्थदीपनी नाम विनयट्ठकथाय टीकागन्धो, विनयसंगहगन्धो, विनयसंगहस्स टीकागन्धो, अङ्गुत्तरट्ठकथाय नवा टीकागन्धो इति इमे चत्तारो गन्धा परक्कमबाहुनामेन लंकादीपिस्सरेन रञ्ञा आयाचितेन सारिपुत्ताचरियेन कता।

सकटसद्दसत्थस्स पञ्चिका नाम टीकागन्धो अत्तनो मतिया सारिपुत्ताचरियेन कतो।

कङ्खावितरणिया विनयत्थमञ्जूसा नाम टीकागन्धो सुमेधानामत्थेरेन आयाचितेन बुद्धनागाचरियेन कतो।

अभिधानप्पदीपिका नाम गन्धो अत्तनो मतिया चुल्लमोग्गलानाचरियेन[2] कतो।

सुबोधालंकारस्स महासीमा नाम टीका, वुत्तोदयविवरणं चाति इमे द्वे गन्धा अत्तनो मतिया वाचिस्सरेन कता।

खुद्दसिक्खाय सुमङ्गलपसादनी नाम नवो टीकागन्धो सुमङ्गलेन आयाचितेन वाचिस्सरेन कतो।

---

१. नम्प—म० २

२. मोग्ग०—म० १

सम्बन्धचिन्ताटीका, बालावतारो, मोग्गलानब्याकरणस्स टीका चा'ति इमे गन्धा सुमङ्गल-बुद्धमित्त-महाकस्सपसंखातेहि तीहि थेरेहि च धम्मकित्ति नाम उपासकेन वानिच्चाभातु उपासकेन[1] आयाचितेन वा वाचिस्सरेन कता ।

नामरूपपरिच्छेदस्स टीका,[2] पदरूपविभावनं, खेमपकरणस्स टीका, सीमालंकारो, मूलसिक्खाय टीका, रूपारूपविभागो, पच्चयसंगहो चा इति इमे सत्त गन्धा अत्तनो मतिया वाचिस्सरेन कता ।

सच्चसंखेपस्स टीकागन्धो सारिपुत्तनामेन थेरेन आयाचितेन वाचिस्सरेन कता ।

R. 72 अभिधम्मावतारस्स टीका अभिधम्मत्थसंगहस्स टीका चा'ति इमे अत्तनो मतिया सुमङ्गलाचरियेन कतो ।

सारत्थसंगहनामगन्धो अत्तनो मतिया बुद्धपियेन कतो ।

दन्तधातुवण्णना नाम पकरणं लंकादीपिस्सरस्स रञ्ञो सेनापतिआयाचितेन धम्मकित्तिनामाचरियेन कतं ।

जिनचरितं नाम पकरणं अत्तनो मतिया मेधंकराचरियेन कतं ।

जिनालंकारो जिनालंकारस्स टीका अत्तनो मतिया बुद्धरक्खिताचरियेन कता[3] ।

अनागतवंसस्स अट्ठकथा अत्तनो मतिया उपतिस्साचरियेन कता ।

---

१. म० १ पोत्थके नत्थि ।

२. रो० पोत्थके नत्थि ।

३. म० २ पोत्थके – अमतरे नाम

कङ्खावितरणिया लीनत्थपकासिनी नाम टीका, निसन्देहो, धम्मानुसारणी, ञेय्यासन्दति, ञेय्यासन्दतिया टीका, सुमहावतारो, लोकपञ्ञत्तिपकरणं, तथागतुप्पत्तिपकरणं, नलाटधातुवण्णना, सीहळवत्थु, धम्मदीपको, पटिपत्तिसंगहो, विसुद्धिमग्गस्स गण्ठि, अभिधम्मगण्ठि, नेत्तिपकरणस्स गण्ठि, विसुद्धिमग्ग-चुल्लनवटीका, सोतप्पमालिनी, पसादजननी, ओकासलोको, सुबोधालंकारस्स नवटीका इमे चेति वीसति गन्धा अत्तनो मतिया वीसताचरियेहि विसुं कता।

सद्दत्थभेदचिन्ता नाम पकरणं अत्तनो मतिया धम्मसिरीनाचरियेन[1] कतो।

सुमरकूटवण्णनं नाम पकरणं राहुलनामत्थेरेन आयाचितेन वाचिस्सरेन कतं।

सोतत्तगीमहानिदानं नाम पकरणं अत्तनो मतिया चुल्लबुद्धघोसाचरियेन कतं।

मधुरसवाहिनी नाम पकरणं अत्तनो मतिया रट्ठपालाचरियेन कतं।

लिङ्गत्थविवरणं नाम पकरणं अत्तनो मतिया सुभूतचन्दनाचरियेन कतं।

सद्दनीतिपकरणं अत्तनो मतिया अग्गवंसाचरियेन कतं।

न्यासपकरणस्स महाटीका नाम टीका अत्तनो मतिया विमलबुद्धाचरियेन[2] कता।

R. 73 मुखमत्तसारो अत्तनो मतिया गुणसागराचरियेन कतो।

---

१. सद्धं—म० २

२. वचीर—म० २

मुखमत्तसारस्स टीका सुतसम्पन्नकयच्वानामेन धम्म-राजिनो[1] गुरूसंघत्थेरेन आयाचितेन गुणसागराचरियेन कता।

सद्दत्थभेदचिन्ताय महाटीका अत्तनो मतिया अभया-चरियेन कता।

लिङ्गत्थविवरणपकासकं नाम पकरणं अत्तनो मतिया ञानसागराचरियेन कतं।

गूळ्हत्थटीका बालप्पबोधनं च इति दुविधं पकरणं अत्तनो मतिया अञ्ञतराचरियेन कतं।

सद्दत्थभेदचिन्ताय मज्झिमटीका अत्तनो मतिया अञ्ञतरा-चरियेन कता।

बालावतारस्स टीका च अत्तनो मतिया उत्तमाचरियेन कता।

सद्दत्थभेदचिन्ताय नवाटीका अत्तनो मतिया अञ्ञतरा-चरियेन कता।

अभिधानप्पदीपिकाय टीका, दण्डीपकरणस्स मगधभूता टीका चा'ति दुविधा टीकायो अत्तनो मतिया सीहसूरनामरञ्ञो एकेन अमच्चेन कता।

कोलद्धजनस्स टीका पासादिकेन नाम थेरेन आयाचितेन चा तेनेव अमच्चेन कता।

कारिका नाम पकरणं ञानगम्भीरनामेन भिक्खुना आया-चितेन धम्मसेनापताचरियेन कता।

एतिमासमिदीपनी नाम पकरणं मनोहारं च अत्तनो मतिया तेनेव धम्मसेनापताचरियेन कतं।

कारिकाय टीका अत्तनो मतिया अञ्ञतराचरियेन कता।

१. राजिनो म० १

एतिमासमिदीपिकाय टीका अत्तनो मतिया अञ्ञतराचरियेन कता।

सद्दविन्दुपकरणं च परमत्थविन्दुपकरणं च अत्तनो मतिया क्यच्वा नाम रञ्ञा[1] कता।

सद्दवुत्तिपकासकं[2] नाम पकरणं अञ्ञतरेन भिक्खुना आयाचितेन सद्धम्मगुरूना नामाचरियेन कतं।

सद्दवुत्तिपकासकस्स टीका अत्तनो मतिया सारिपुत्ताचरियेन कता।

R. 74 कच्चायनसारो च कच्चायनभेदं च[3] कच्चायनसारस्स टीका चा'ति तिविधं[4] पकरणं अत्तनो मतिया धम्मानन्दाचरियेन[5] कतं।

लोकदीपकसारं नाम पकरणं अत्तनो मतिया नवेन मेधंकराचरियेन कतं।

लोकुप्पत्तिपकरणं अत्तनो मतिया अग्गपण्डिताचरियेन कतं।

जङ्घदासकस्स मगधभूता टीका अत्तनो मतिया वजिराचरियेन[6] कता।

मातिकट्ठदीपनी, अभिधम्मत्थसंगहवण्णना, सीमालंकारस्स टीका, गण्ढिसारो, पट्ठानगणनानयो चा'ति इमे पञ्च पकरणानि अत्तनो मतिया सद्धम्मजोतिपालाचरियेन कता।

---

१. धम्मराजस्स गुरूना अञ्ञतराचरियेन कतं—म० २

२. नं—म० २

३. म० २ पोत्थके नत्थि।

४. दुविधं—म० २

५. अञ्ञतरा०—म० २

६. चीवराचीबरेन—म० २

संखेपवण्णना परक्कमबाहुनामेन जम्बुदीपस्सरेन रञ्ञा आयाचितेनेव सद्धम्मजोतिपालाचरियेन कता।

कच्चायनस्स सुत्तनिद्देसो अत्तनो सिस्सेन धम्मचारित्थेरेन आयाचितेन सद्धम्मजोतिपालाचरियेन कतो।

विनयसमुट्ठानदीपनी नाम पकरणं अत्तनो गुरूना संघत्थेरेन आयाचितेनेव सद्धम्मजोतिपालाचरियेन कता।

सत्त पकरणानि पन तेन पुक्कामनगरे[1] कतानि, संखेपवण्णना येव लंकादीपे कता।

अभिधम्मपण्णरसट्ठानवण्णनं नाम पकरणं अत्तनो मतिया नवेन विमलबुद्धाचरियेन कतं।

सद्दसारत्थजालिनी नाम पकरणं अत्तनो मतिया नागीताचरियेन[2] कता।

सद्दसारत्थजालिनिया टीका पन्यनगरे रञ्ञो गुरूना संघराजेन आयाचितेन तेनेव विमलबुद्धाचरियेन कता।

वुत्तोदयस्स टीका, अभिधम्मत्थसंगहस्स टीकाय परमत्थ-
मञ्जूसा नाम अनुटीका, दसगण्ढिवण्णना नाम पकरणं, मगधभूतं
R. 75 विदग्गं, विदधिमुखमण्डनस्स[3] टीका चाति इमानि पञ्च[4] पकर-
णानि अत्तनो मतिया तेनेव नवेन वेपुल्लबुद्धाचरियेन कता।[5]

---

१. मुक्का—म० २

२. नागितेन—म० १

३. मण्डस्स—म० १

४. चत्तारि—म० २

५. विमलँ—म० २

पञ्चपकरणटीकाय नवानुटीका अत्तनो मतिया अञ्ञतराचरियेन कता।

मणिसारमञ्जूसा नाम अनुटीका मणिदीपं नाम द्वारकथाय अनुटीका जातकविसोधनं च गण्डाभरणं च अत्तनो मतिया अरियवंसाचरियेन कता।

पेटकोपदेसस्स टीका अत्तनो मतिया उदुम्बरनामाचरियेन मकुवनगरे[1] कता।

चतुभाणवारस्स अट्ठकथा, महासारपकासिनी, महादीपनी, सारत्थदीपनी, गतिपकरणं, हत्थसारो, भूम्मसंगहो, भूम्मनिद्देसो, दसवत्थु, कायविरतिटीका, जोतना, निरूत्ति, विभत्तिकथा, सद्धम्मपालिनी, पञ्चगतिवण्णना, बालचित्तपबोधनं, धम्मचक्कसुत्तस्स नवट्ठकथा, दन्तधातुपकरणस्स टीका च सद्धम्मपायनो, बालप्पबोधनटीका च जिनालंकारस्स नवटीका च लिङ्गत्थविवरणविनिच्छयो, पातिमोक्खविवरणं, परमत्थकथाविवरणं, समन्तपासादिकाविवरणं, चतुभागट्ठकथाविवरणं, अभिधम्मत्थसंगहविवरणं, सच्चसंखेपविवरणं, सद्दत्थभेदचिन्ताविवरणं, सद्दवुत्तिविवरणं, कच्चायनसारविवरणं, अभिधम्मसंगहस्स टीकाविवरणं, महावेस्सन्तरजातकस्स-विवरणं, सक्काभिमतं महावेस्सन्तरजातकस्स नवट्ठकथा, पठमसम्बोधि, लोकनीति, बुद्धघोसाचरियनिदानं, मिलिन्दपण्हावण्णना, चतुरक्खाय अट्ठकथा, सद्दवुत्तिपकरणस्स नवटीका चाति इमानि चत्तालीसपकरणानि अत्तनो मतिया सासनस्स जुतिया च सद्धम्मस्स ठितिया च लंकादीपादीसु विसुं विसुं आचरियेहि कतानि।

---

१. पकुतो—म० २

सम्बुद्धे गाथा च-ल-नवहारगुणवण्णना चाति इमे बुद्धपणामादिका गाथायो अत्तनो अत्तनो बुद्धगुणपकासनत्थाय अत्तनो परेसं च अनन्तपञ्ञापवत्तनत्थाय च पण्डितेहि लंकादीपादीसु ठानेसु विसुं विसुं कता ।

इति चुल्लगन्धवंसे गन्धकारकाचरियदीपको नाम

चतुत्थो परिच्छेदो ।

पञ्चमो परिच्छेदो

पकिण्णक दीपको

१. धम्मक्खन्धनामदीपना

R.76 **नामं आरोपनं पोट्ठं, फलं गन्धकारस्स च।**
लेखं लेखापनं चेव, वदामि अहं तद अनन्तरं ति॥

तत्थ चतुरासीतिधम्मक्खन्धसहस्सानं[1] पिटकानिकायङ्ग-वग्गनिपातादिकं नामं।

केन आरोपितं, किं अत्थं आरोपितं ति।

तत्रायं विसज्जना। केन आरोपितं ति, पञ्चसतेहि खीणासवेहि महाकस्सप पमुखेहि आरोपितं। ते हि सम्बद्धवचनं संगायन्ति—इदं पिटकं, अयं निकायो, इदं अङ्गं, वग्गो, अयं निदानो, इति एवं आदिकं नामं कारापेन्ति।[2]

कत्थ आरोपितं ति, राजगहे वेभारपब्बतस्स पादे धम्म-मण्डपे आरोपितं।

कदा आरोपितं ति, भगवतो परिनिब्बुते पठमसंगायनकाले आरोपितं तिके मासे निक्खमनिये।

किमत्थं आरोपितं ति, धम्मक्खन्धानं अनट्ठाय सत्तहिताय वोहारसुखत्थाय च आरोपितं।

---

१. सहस्सानि—म० २
२. करोन्ति—म० २

संगीतिकाले पञ्चसता खीणासवा तेसं च धम्मक्खन्धानं नामवग्गनिपातका। इमस्स धम्मक्खन्धस्स अयं नामो होतु, इमस्स पकरणस्स अयं नामो इति अब्रवुं, सब्बनामादिकं किच्चं अकंसु।[1]

धम्मक्खन्धनामदीपना निट्ठिता।

२. गन्धकरलेखेलेखापनानिसंसदीपना

चतुरासीतिधम्मक्खन्धसहस्सानि केन पोत्थके आरोपितानि, कत्थ आरोपितानि, कदा आरोपितानि, किं अत्थं आरोपितानि, अयं पुच्छा। तत्रायं विसज्जना।

केन आरोपितानीति, खीणासवमहानागेहि आरोपितानि।

कत्थ आरोपितानि, लंकादीपे आरोपितानि।

कदा आरोपितानि, सद्धातिस्सराजिनो पुत्तस्स वट्टगामणि-राजस्स काले आरोपितानि।

किं अत्थं आरोपितानि, धम्मक्खन्धानं अविधसंनत्थाय सद्धम्मठितिया सत्तहिताय आरोपितानि।[2]

---

1. ते खीणासवा यदि नामादिकं किच्चं अकतं न सुपाकतं तस्मा वोहारसुखत्थाय नामादिकं किच्चं अनागते धपिरक्खाय (?) नामादिकं पवत्तितं असंजानामानो सुट्ठु पाकतो सब्बसो चावेति। —म० 2

2. धरमानो भगवा अम्हाकं सुगतो धरो।
निकाये पञ्च देसेसि याव निब्बानगमना॥ 1॥
सब्बे पि ते भिक्खू आदि मनसा वचसा मरो (?)।
सब्बे वाचुग्गता होन्ति महापञ्ञासतिरो ?॥ 2॥
निब्बुते लोकनाथम्हि, भतो (?) वस्ससतं भवे।
अरिया नरिया पि च, सब्बे वाचुग्गता ध्रुवं॥ 3॥
ततो परं अट्ठारसं, द्विसतं वस्सगणनं।
सब्बे पुथुज्जना चेव, अरिया च सब्बे पि ते॥ 4॥

R 78 यो कोचि पण्डितो वीरो अट्ठकथादिकं गन्धं करोति कारापेति वा तस्स अनन्तको होति पुञ्ञसंचयो, अनन्तको होति पुञ्ञानिसंसो चतुरासीतिचेतियसहस्सकरणसदिसो चतुरासीति-

---

मनसा वचसा येव, वाचुग्गता सब्बदा ।
दुट्ठगामनीरञ्ञो च, कालो वाचुग्गतो धुवं ।
अरियानरिया पि च, निकारे धारणं सदा (?) ॥ 5 ॥
ततो परंहि राजा वं, ततो चुतो च तुसिते ।
उप्पज्जि देवलोके च, देवेहि परिवारितो ॥ 6 ॥
सद्धातिस्सो 'ति नामेन, तस्स किं निनिकोहि तो ? ।
तकोलद्धरट्ठो होति, बुद्धसासनंपालको ॥ 7 ॥
तदा काले भिक्खु, आसि सब्बे वाचुग्गता सदा ।
निकाये पञ्चविधे व, यावा रञ्ञो मनणा ॥ 8 ॥
ततो चुतो स राजा, च तुसिते उप्पज्जति ।
देवलोके ठितो सन्तो, तदा वाचुग्गता ततो ॥ 9 ॥
तस्स पुत्ता पि अहेसुं, अनेका व रज्जं गता ।
अनुक्कमेन चुता ते, देवलोकम्हि सता धुवं ॥ 10 ॥
तथा पि ते सब्बे, भिक्खू वाचुग्गता' व सम्पदा ? ।
निकाये पञ्चविधे व, धारणा व सतिमता ? ॥ 11 ॥
ततो परं पोत्थकेसु, निकाया पञ्च पि ठिता ।
तदा अट्ठकथा टीका, सब्बे गन्धा पोत्थके गता ॥ 12 ॥
सन्बे पोट्ठेसु ये गन्धा, पाळे-अट्ठकथाटीका ।
संठिता संठिता होन्ति, सब्बे पि नो नस्सन्ति ते ॥ 13 ॥
तदा ते पोट्ठके येव, निकाया पि ठिताखिला ।
तदा अट्ठकथादीनि, भवन्तीति वदन्ति च ॥ 14 ॥
परिहारो पण्डितेहि, वत्तवो, व......... ।
लंकादीपिस्सरञ्ञो व, सद्धातिस्सस्स राजिनो ॥ 15 ॥
वुत्तलंकादीपिस्स, इस्सरो धम्मिको धरो ।
तदा खीणासवस्स राजिनो पुत्त लंकादीपिस्स
इस्सरो धम्मिको धरो ॥ 16 ॥

बुद्धरूपकरणसदिसो चतुरासीतिबोधिरूक्खसहस्सरोपनसदिसो चतुरासीतिविहारसहस्सकरणसदिसो ।

यो च बुद्धवचनमञ्जूसं करोति वा कारापेति वा, (सो च बुद्धवचनं करोति वा करापेति वा)[1], यो च बुद्धवचनं पोत्थके लेखं करोति वा कारापेति वा, यो च पोत्थकं वा पोत्थकमूलं वा देति वा दापेति वा, यो च तेलं वा चुण्णं वा धञ्ञं वा (पोत्थकपुञ्छनत्थाय यं किञ्चि नवत्तं (?) पोत्थकछिद्दे अनिट्ठाय (?) यं किञ्चि सुत्तं वा)[2] कट्ठफलकद्वयं पोत्थकं वूहनत्थाय यं किञ्चि वत्तं वा पोत्थकबन्धनत्थाय यं किञ्चि योत्तं (वा पोत्थकलापपूतनत्थाय यं किञ्चि तविकं ?[3]) देति वा दापेति वा यो च हरितालेन वा मनोसिलाय वा सुवण्णेन वा रजतेन वा पोत्थकमण्डनं वा कट्ठफलकमण्डनं वा करोति वा कारापेति वा तस्स अनन्तको होति पुञ्ञसंचयो, अनन्तको होति पुञ्ञानिसंसो, चतुरासीतिचेतियसहस्सकरणसदिसो, चतुरासीतिविहारसहस्सकरणसदिसो, भवे निवत्तमानो सो सीलगुणं उपागतो महातेजो सदा होति सोहनादो विसारदो ।

तदा खीणासवा सब्बे ओलोकेन्ति अनागता ।
खीणासवा पस्सन्ति ते, दुवञ्ञे व पुथुज्जनो ? ॥
सब्बे पि ते भिक्खू, आदि बहुतरा पुथुज्जना ।
न सिक्खिसन्ति ते पञ्च, निकाये वाचुग्गतं ति ॥ 17 ॥
पोट्ठकेसु सब्बे पञ्च, आरोधपन्ति खीणासवा ।
खद्धम्मचिरठितत्थाय, जनानं पुञ्ञत्थाय च ॥ 18 ॥

1. म० 1 पोत्थके नत्थि ।

2. म० 1 पोत्थके नत्थि ।

3. म० 1 पोत्थके नत्थि

आयुवण्णबलुपेतो, धम्मकामो भवे सदा ।
देवमनुस्सलोकेसु, महेसक्खो अनामयो ॥ १ ॥

भवे निवत्तमानो सो, पञ्ञवा सुसमाहितो ।
अधिपच्चपरिवारो, सब्बसुखाधिगच्छति ॥ २ ॥

सद्धो विहारी हदयञ्ञू[1], स विहगतो भवे ।
अङ्गपच्चङ्गसंपन्नो, आरोहोपरिनाह वा ॥ ३ ॥

सब्बसत्तप्पियो लोके, सब्बत्थ पूजितो भवे ।
देवमनुस्ससंचरो, मित्तसहायपालितो ॥ ४ ॥

देवमनुस्ससंपत्ति, अनुभोति पुनप्पुनं ।
अरहत्तफलं पत्तो, निब्बानं पापुणिस्सति ॥ ५ ॥

पटिसम्भिदा चतस्सो, अभिञ्ञा छब्बिधे वरे ।
विमोक्खे अट्ठके सेट्ठे, गमिस्सति अनागते ॥ ६ ॥

तस्मा हि पण्डितो पोसो, सम्पस्सं हितं अत्तनो ।
कारेय्य सामं गन्धे च, अञ्ञे हि प कारापये ॥ ७ ॥

पोट्ठके च गन्धे, पाळिअट्ठकथादिके ।
धम्ममञ्जूसा गन्धे च, लेखं करे कारापये ॥ ८ ॥

पोट्ठकं पोट्ठकमूलं च, तेलं चुण्णथूसं पि च ।
पिलोतिकादिकं सुत्तं, कट्ठफलद्वयं पि[2] च ॥ ९ ॥

---

1. हदञ्ञू—म० 2
2. ०ट्ठयम्हि—म० 2

धम्मपूतनत्थाय[1] च, यं किञ्चि महग्घवत्तं ।
धम्मबन्धनयोत्तं च, यं किञ्चि ठपितं पि[2] ।। १० ।।

ददेय्य धम्मवत्तं पि, विप्पसन्नेन चेतसा ।
अञ्ञे चापि दज्जापेय्य, मित्तसहायबन्धवे' ति ।। ११ ।।

गन्धकरलेखेलेखापनानिसंसदीपना निट्ठिता ।

इति चुल्लगन्धवंसे पकिण्णकदीपको नाम पञ्चमो परिच्छेदो ।

---

1. ०मदन—म० 2
2. च—म० 2

लेखक परिचयो

सो [1]हंसारट्ठजातो, नन्दपञ्ञो'ति विस्सुतो ।
सद्धासीलविरूपेतो, धम्मसारगवेसनो[2] ॥
सो यं ।[3]
सन्तिसभावं निब्बानं, गवेसन्तो पुनप्पुनं ।
वसन्तो[4] तं मनोरम्मं[5], पिटकत्तयसंगहं ।
गन्धवंसं इमं खुद्दं, निस्साय[6] जङ्घदासकं'ति ॥

इति पामोज्जत्थायारञ्ञवासिना नन्दपञ्ञाचरियेन कतो चुल्लगन्धवंसो निट्ठितो ।

---

1. म० 1 पोत्थके नत्थि ।
2. रस—म० 2
3. अहं म० 1; म० 2—
   भोगं ताविधं ।
   जिननुवयं पूरं सब्बधम्मं विचिनन्तो ।
   विसति मिस्सं गतो ॥
   सब्बधम्मविस्सज्जन्तो किकारणेव भिक्खुनो ।
   छवस्साहं गनं भित्वा कामानं अभिमद्दनं ॥
4. अरञ्ञविहारे—म० 1; गवेसन्तो—म० 2
5. वनारम्मं—म० 2
6. अभिय संघे—म०2

अनुक्कमणिका

(१) गाथा-पठम-पाद-अनुक्कमणिका

(२) विसेस-सद्द-अनुक्कमणिका

स